Sex
Energy

BOOKS BY ROBERT S. DE ROPP

Sex Energy

The Sexual Force in Man and Animals

ROBERT S. DE ROPP

A SEYMOUR LAWRENCE BOOK
DELACORTE PRESS / N.Y.

Grateful acknowledgment is made to the following
for permission to quote
from material already published.

KING SOLOMON'S RING by Konrad Z. Lorenz, translated by
Marjorie Latzke: Copyright 1952 by the publishers, Thomas
Y. Crowell Company, New York. Used by permission of
Thomas Y. Crowell Company and Methuen & Company, Ltd.

THE LIFE OF THE BEE by Maurice Maeterlinck, translated by
Alfred Sutro: Used by permission of Dodd, Mead & Company
and George Allen and Unwin Ltd.

MY LIFE AND LOVES by Frank Harris: Copyright © 1925 by
Frank Harris. Copyright © 1953 by Nellie Harris. Copyright
© 1963 by Arthur Leonard Ross as executor of the Frank
Harris estate. Used by permission of Grove Press, Inc.

PATTERNS OF SEXUAL BEHAVIOR by Clellan S. Ford and Frank
A. Beach: Copyright 1951 by Clellan Stearns Ford and Frank
Ambrose Beach. Reprinted by permission of Harper & Row,
Publishers.

SEX IN HISTORY by G. Rattray Taylor: Reprinted by permission
of the publisher, The Vanguard Press, from SEX IN HISTORY
by G. Rattray Taylor. Copyright © 1954 by G. Rattray
Taylor. Used by permission of Thames and Hudson Ltd.

THE SEX LIFE OF THE ANIMALS by Herbert Wendt: Copyright
© 1965 by Simon & Schuster, Inc. Original German language
edition copyright © 1962 by Rowohlt Verlag Gmbh Reinbek
Bei Hamburg. Reprinted by permission of Simon & Schuster,
Inc. and George Weidenfeld & Nicolson Ltd.

DRAWINGS BY *Eloise Vogt*
TECHNICAL ILLUSTRATIONS BY *Magnuson and Vincent, Inc.*

Contents

III. SEX ENERGY DEIFIED   113

IV. SEX ENERGY DEGRADED   155

Illustrations

I.
BIG SEX
AND
LITTLE SEX

TWO ASPECTS OF EROS

SEX ENERGY . . . the compelling force behind erotic rites, the bacchanals, the Floralia, the feasts of Priapus and Aphrodite. Sex energy . . . manifesting itself in perverted orgies, in gross extravagances of cruelty and lust from the secret indulgences of Tiberius on Capri to the fantasied atrocities in the brain of the Marquis de Sade. Sex energy . . . fettered, distorted, denied its normal outlet, generating guilt, fear, horror, persecution, the host of sickly delusions that haunted our devil-ridden ancestors and even today continue to plague their descendants. Sex energy . . . soaring, beautified, etherealized, a spiritual flame uniting two in one, transcending the flesh, a symbol of mystical blending. Sex energy . . . a universal biological urge with no other function than to bring about the union of the gametes, the active moving sperm of the male, the large inactive egg cell of the female.

All this and a good deal more is implied in the term sex energy. It spreads out, like an amoeba, in all directions, transcends the purely biological, enters the realms of art, pathology, religion, morals, ethics, metaphysics. It shows itself in everything, even in the structure of some languages with their "male" nouns and "female" nouns. If the mind of contemporary man seems obsessed by this force let us admit that there is reason for the obsession. For nature herself is sex-obsessed. If there is one mechanism we can be almost certain of finding in any form of life we choose to study it is the sexual mechanism. Even bacteria have a sexual function of a sort. Even viruses

3

. . . Eros and Aphrodite are everywhere and in everything.

Let us be more specific. This talk of Eros and Aphrodite is premature. We have to distinguish two different sexual phenomena. First there is micro-sex. This is almost universal. Cellular sex or *nuclear* sex is micro. It concerns two cells, which biologists call gametes, whose distinguishing feature is that they carry only one-half of the genetic code. The gametes are usually, not always, different in size. The small, active, wriggling member we traditionally call male or sperm. The large passive member we call female, egg or ovum. But micro-sex may be even subcellular, consisting of an exchange of portions of genetic material such as occurs among viruses and bacteria. We might argue that, at this point, the phenomenon ceases to be sexual at all, insisting that the essence of sex is maleness and femaleness and that mere exchanges of bits of genetic material do not qualify for the sexual label. It is a question of semantics.

In any case, *micro-sex* (small sex) is the biological foundation of *macro-sex* (big sex). About this there can be no argument whatever. All sexual phenomena in nature are designed to produce one result, a blending of the genetic codes of two members of the same species. The glow and sparkle of sex as we humans experience it, the cuddling, kissing, copulating, tumescence, orgasm, all serve one purpose only. They set the stage for a cellular drama that involves the sperm's odyssey through the tunnels and portals of the female genital tract, its quest for the waiting egg, its union with this egg. All this occurs after the sweating lovers have lost interest in each other, are wrapped in sleep, their pulse rates back to normal, or have dressed and resumed their usual occupations. They have merely been instrumental in setting in motion the micro-sexual drama, of which they are as little aware as they are of events in some remote galaxy. Of course, if the micro-drama has been performed successfully (if the sperm has found and united with the waiting egg), this unawareness will be replaced, in the female at least, by a very acute awareness of a change in her condition, a change summarized in the words (spoken with triumph or horror, disgust or delight, depending on circumstances): "I'm expecting a baby."

So when we talk about sex energy we must differentiate between the energy of macro-sex, which brings about the union of male and female, man and woman, mare and stallion, cock and hen, buck and doe, and the energy of micro-sex, which joins the male gamete with the female gamete. The orders of magnitude are quite different. So are the forces involved.

We will start with small things and work toward larger ones. Micro-sex may not seem very romantic. It does not form the subject of novels, ballads or poems (except for one rare micro-sexual epic of Aldous Huxley's beginning: "A thousand million spermatozoa, all of them alive."). But for one not totally preoccupied with moonlight and roses, this micro-drama may appear even more astonishing than the macro-phenomena that so excite poets and novelists, not to mention sexologists, psychologists, psychopathologists and self-styled protectors of public morals. In any case it would be biologically most unsound to describe the energies that underlie macro-sex without first giving an account of the underlying micro-phenomena. For without the micro-phenomena there simply would not be any macro-sex, no girls, no boys, no pining Juliets nor priapic Romeos. The whole species would perish.

IN THE BEGINNING

Start at the start. Visualize the transition from azoic (the lifeless) to archeozoic (the dawn of life). Here spins a life-free earth still hot from creation, simmering under the rays of a younger sun. Its surface is covered in cloud, its atmosphere thick with steam. Oxygen, for us so vital, is probably absent from that atmosphere but there is plenty of chemical activity even without the oxygen. Bombarded with radiation from the juvenile sun the primordial seas are bubbling like cauldrons of stew. Methane, ammonia, carbon dioxide, phosphates are all present in the water. Powerful radiations strike the molecules, raising their component atoms to a frenzy of excitation. Randomly and ceaselessly the deluge of solar energy plays with the molecules of this primordial stew, combining, recombining, while the oceans gradually cool and the vapors condense.

For how long did this random activity continue? A billion years? Two billion? We have no way of knowing. The time span was prodigious. Given that enormous time span we may, without offending against what are loosely called the laws of probability, assume that all sorts of odd chemicals were formed without the intervention of a deity or any guiding principle, but simply by accident. Such, in any case, is the view preferred by those who consider themselves qualified to speak on the subject of the creation of life.

Purpose or no purpose, God or no God, the likelihood remains that somewhere in that primordial stew some very odd chemicals did form and these odd chemicals became the framework on which all that we call life was later constructed. Their peculiarities also provided the basis for all micro-sexual phenomena. So, though we may know nothing of chemistry, it is only fitting that we look at these chemicals, for without them there would be neither love nor life.

THE CODE OF LIFE

Several new concepts have revolutionized man's thinking in the twentieth century. Among these is the idea of life as a self-perpetuating code. A fertile idea. It enabled students of life to discard a host of hazy definitions and to define with precision the central problem of the science of life. The idea initiated some of the most fruitful research of the century, research performed not in a blaze of publicity with monstrous atom-smashers costing millions of dollars but quietly and dis-

creetly in small laboratories by men whose names are still unfamiliar to the lay public. Though their work does not receive
the publicity accorded to the spectacular and sometimes terrifying exploits of the atomic physicists, it may, in the long
run, prove to be more influential in shaping the destiny of man.
For there can be no doubt in the mind of one properly informed that this research opens the way to the artificial creation of life, to a repetition in the laboratory under the guid-
ance of an intelligent being of those chemical events which
we assume happened purely by accident billions of years ago
in the primordial seas.

So we now will consider the code on which life depends,
the variations of which underlie the rich multiplicity of living
things and to which all sexual processes, micro and macro,
are ultimately linked. Going back to the primordial stew we
have to suppose that at some time or other an extraordinary
molecule developed. It was immensely long and shaped like
a ladder twisted into a spiral. Each rung of the ladder was
made up of a pair of molecules belonging to the class of substances called purines or pyrimidines. There were only four
of these substances (a modest alphabet with which the whole
story of life was to be written). Their names (and the reader
may as well know them, for they spell out life itself) were
adenine, guanine, cytosine and thymine, AGCT for short. The
rungs of the ladder were made up of the two short molecules,
thymine or cytosine, linked to the two longer molecules, adenine or guanine. They were linked in pairs, A to T, G to C.
The spiral sides of the ladder were made of a sugar called
deoxyribose and a molecule of phosphoric acid. The whole
assemblage was labeled by the chemists with the formidable
name deoxyribonucleic acid, which, in laboratory shorthand,
was abbreviated to DNA. (Fig. 1).

The DNA code in living things as we know them today must
be twice translated if the process of life is to occur. The first
translation is into the four-letter ribonucleic acid (RNA) code
in which the letter T (thymine) was replaced by the letter U

(uracil). The second translation is into the twenty-letter amino acid code. On a long molecule called messenger RNA the twenty amino acids are linked together to form proteins (enzymes) which provide the basis for all chemical processes in living organisms. These enzymes catalyze the chemical reactions which supply the energy for the various manifestations of life.

So we can depict the simplest of living things as a collection of giant code molecules written in three alphabets, the four letters of the DNA code (AGCT), the four letters of the RNA code (AGCU), and the twenty letters of the protein code. The DNA was the core of this archetypal living thing, the RNA surrounded the core, and the protein provided an outer coating. Such an entity could only exist in the free form in those primordial seas which were presumably full of all sorts of organic substances formed by direct chemical interactions.

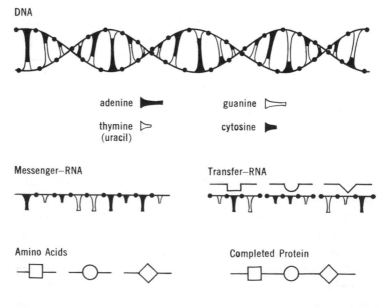

1. The code of life.

Such primitive living entities cannot be found in our contemporary oceans. If they did exist or were formed by accident, they would rapidly be destroyed by today's microorganisms. But the viruses, which can only multiply within living cells, resemble our archetypes in this respect, that they have only a few code molecules (RNA or DNA but not both) plus a protein overcoat. As scientists see the act of creation today it must have started with the formation of entities similar to the viruses.

PRIMORDIAL SEX

If the coded DNA molecule was the foundation of life what was the foundation of sex? To this question we can offer a fairly simple reply. The basis of sex was a blending of DNA codes. Obviously such a blending might offer advantages. It would produce an entity with greater "word power," an increased capacity to synthesize new molecules. We can think of archetype A with a twenty-word code and archetype B with a twenty-five-word code (in terms of the number of proteins they were able to synthesize). If the two had twenty "codons" in common then a combination of A and B would yield a new entity having a vocabulary of twenty-five words, which, if we take the view that increase in complexity is tantamount to progress, would represent a forward step. Or, to put it in terms more acceptable to a Darwinian, the organism with the larger code might have an advantage in the struggle for existence.

Thus we can visualize, in those soupy primordial seas, the dawn of the sexual phenomenon as a blending of DNA codes brought about (as we must assume the whole of life was brought about, unless we postulate some guiding force or deity), by entirely random collisions of those primitive particles whose dimensions, we must assume, were well beyond the reach of the optical microscope. The primitive sexual process, we must conclude, was rather similar to the process of feeding. One organism in a sense devoured another. But whereas the feeding process results in the destruction of the food by the feeder, the sexual process results in the blending of two codes into one. The resulting new code combines characteristics of both parent codes.

Time passed, eon after eon. Random blendings continued. Codes grew ever more complex. The final result was the living cell as we know it today. In such a cell the DNA code is usually confined to a special part of the cell known as the nucleus. Furthermore, in most organisms, this master code is concentrated into a specific number of threadlike entities which their discoverers called chromosomes (colored bodies) because of the high affinity they had for certain dyes.

The basis of micro-sex is the blending of codes. This can occur in various ways, some of them quite unfamiliar and peculiar. Not all of them are truly sexual, not all of them are beneficial. The viruses, for example, can only exist by blending their codes with those of higher organisms. A virus particle enters a cell, blends its code with the code of the cell and forces that cell to make virus particles instead of attending to its own affairs. The cell may make so many virus particles that it perishes in the process. Or it may retain the viral code as part of its own and operate somewhat abnormally as a result. There is more and more evidence accumulating to suggest that cancer cells may behave in the way they do because they carry foreign genetic material introduced by some virus. This foreign material upsets the very delicate mechanism by which the organism controls the multiplication of its cells. The cancer cells multiply and invade the rest of the body, thereby bringing about their own demise as well as the death of their host.

HARMONIOUS BLENDINGS

This should convince the discerning reader that micro-sex, from the beginning, posed a certain threat. The blending of codes would be in no sense beneficial if the instructions contained in one code were hopelessly at variance with the instructions contained in the other. The result would merely be confusion, or the destruction of a more complex organism by a simpler one, such as happens when a virus invades a cell and compels it to manufacture virus particles. We must assume that, during the evolution of micro-sex, a lot of blending did occur which was in no way beneficial and merely led to confusion of both the codes involved. Gradually, by a process of selection, organisms developed mechanisms that prevented this random blending of dissimilar codes. The foundation of micro-sex was laid. It made possible the blending of codes only within certain limits. The codes had to be similar in many respects. If they were too different they would not blend.

This is the fundamental law of micro-sex and it underlies all our classifications of living things. All members of a *race* or *breed* within a species have codes sufficiently similar to allow blending. Members of different *species* within a *genus* have codes that are similar but not similar enough to permit blending. There are exceptions. The code of the ass is sufficiently similar to that of the horse to permit them to be blended to give a mule. The mule, however, is sterile and would become extinct but for human intervention. Members of different *genera* have codes so different that no blending is possible.

The viruses, of course, continued to violate this law, penetrating the cells of totally foreign organisms by a sort of parody of the fertilization process and compelling those cells to produce fresh virus particles to their own great detriment. Nor can we doubt that these maleficent obligatory parasites, whose own codes are so defective that they can only reproduce with the help of another cell, would have brought the evolution of life to a grinding halt had not their hosts developed certain defenses that allowed them at least to limit the ravages of this almost universal enemy. (It is curious to note that the two chief threats to the continuation of life on earth, man and viruses, have now joined forces. Men have learned to make new viruses and concern has been voiced by some very prominent workers in this field that these new viruses, against which living things will have no protection, may escape from the laboratories with disastrous results. "It seems almost indecent to hint that, so far as the advance of medicine is concerned, molecular biology is an evil thing." This from Sir Macfarlane Burnet, Nobel Prize winner and leading virologist, writing in the *Lancet.*)

The capacity to distinguish between genetic codes became, at an early stage, the characteristic of micro-sex. *Some* differences were acceptable. There would be no evolutionary advantage in the sexual process if only identical codes could blend. But the differences had to be held within certain strict limits. The DNA strands of the organisms had to be of the same length and had to contain the same amount of information. There could be slight differences in the wording of the message. The word "white" could be substituted for the word "black," but the general "sense" of the message had to be the same.

So the great law of micro-sex, that like must blend with like, was established early in the evolutionary process. How was this blending brought about? It was brought about in a variety of ways, some of which we must assume have long been abandoned. Today we can only study the techniques that have survived. The basic sexual concept of male and female is not applicable to all of these unions. The common bread mold, for instance, grows in the form of a mass of microscopic threads collectively known as a mycelium. That these threads are of two different kinds can be easily proved.

If we grow them next to each other they come together and at the point of union they produce a special kind of black spore (called a zygospore from the Greek word *zygotos*, yoked) in which a blending of genetic codes has taken place. This is a sexual process but we cannot call the uniting threads male and female. For we have to insist that the characteristic of the male is that it *seeks out and penetrates* the female and that the female is penetrated by the male. But in our bread mold neither partner penetrates nor is penetrated. There is simply a blending of DNA from each thread in the knobbly interior of the black zygospore (Fig. 2). There is a difference in the threads. If we call one plus and the other minus then we can show that a plus will not fuse with a plus nor a minus with a minus. But to call one male and the other female would be meaningless.

The bread mold is not the only living thing in which we can say that sex exists without distinction of male and female. A little one-celled green alga (Chlamydomonas) which can easily be found swimming about in pond water, mates from time to time as the bread mold mates. Two individuals of the

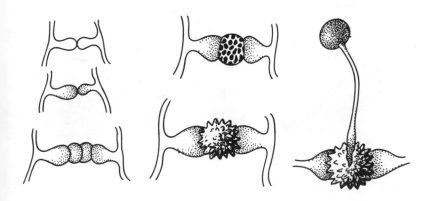

2. *Sexual union in the bread mold. We cannot call the uniting threads either male or female.*

same size come together and fuse (Fig. 3a). One can call this a sexual union but one cannot label one cell male and the other female. Another small swimmer (Pandorina) is very like Chlamydomonas but it produces mating cells of two different sizes. They both swim freely but one is about twice as big as

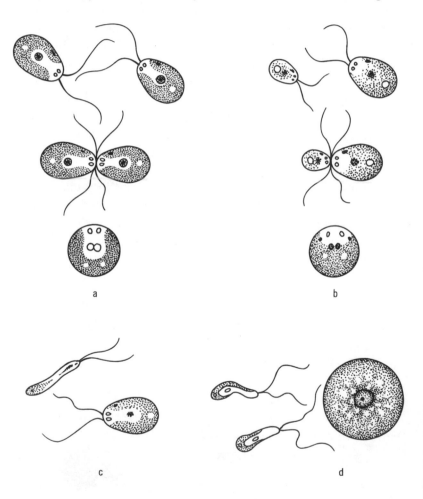

a   b

c   d

3. *Sexual union in (a) Chlamydomonas, (b) Pandorina, (c) Eudorina, (d) Volvox. At this point Eros and Aphrodite have entered the stage of life.*

the other (Fig. 3b). Yet another one-celled swimmer (Eudorina) produces mating cells that are even more different in size. Still they are both free-swimming and we cannot justifiably call one male and one female. We call them both gametes ("marrying cells" from the Greek word for marriage), and we call the small one a *microgamete* and the big one a *macrogamete* (Fig. 3c). Finally, in our drop of pond water, we may find a beautiful globular green entity composed of a whole mass of cells united together, rolling along by the combined action of threadlike appendages or flagella. This alga is called Volvox. It is many-celled and produces two kinds of sex cells, one large, spherical and immobile, the other small and active (Fig. 3d). Without hesitation we tag the big spherical cell with the female label and call it an egg cell or ovum. The little active swimmer we call male, a typical sperm. Volvox satisfies all our criteria. The active sperm seeks out and penetrates the passive egg. Eros and Aphrodite have entered the stage of life, at least on the micro scale. But observe. This male-female dichotomy is quite unimportant. The only thing that really matters is the blending of genetic codes. And this is accomplished just as well by our bread mold, with no male or female but only plus or minus, as it is by Volvox with its well-differentiated sperm and egg.

This may lead the reader to conclude that the whole male-female interaction is merely an accidental by-product of evolution and not really necessary at all. Perhaps this is so. The fact remains that the sperm and egg pattern we see in Volvox has been repeated again and again in all sorts of living things, both plant and animal, so presumably the male-female dichotomy offers some advantages from the evolutionary standpoint.

Let us observe, in passing, one very important consequence of the state of affairs that exists in that lovely green globe we call Volvox. It opens the door to *inevitable death*. The spherical colonies reproduce only through their eggs and sperm. They do not split into two as do the simpler forms like Chlamydomonas. The sperm unites with the egg within the hollow sphere (a curious and senseless pattern of reproduction because it ensures that the life code blends only with itself). New colonies develop within the old which ruptures and dies. *Sexual differentiation and inevitable death enter the stage of life together.* Eros and Thanatos begin their strife at the humble level of an alga no bigger than a pin's head.

SINGLE CODE, DOUBLE CODES

We recapitulate briefly. In the beginning was the primary code and the code had four letters (the AGCT of deoxyribonucleic acid). The primary code carried the central genetic message that distinguishes a man from an ass or an ape. The secondary code was a translation from the primary. From the secondary code came the instructions for building proteins for which twenty letters were used. From the activity of proteins (enzymes) all the chemical processes which constitute life arose. What then is life? It is a chemical encyclopedia with a built-in mechanism for self-translation, written in three different languages, the letters of which are different chemical compounds. And what is sex? It is a device for introducing small variations in the translation by combining two codes that differ in *minor respects*. The differences have to be minor. Major differences make blending impossible. This rules out the formation of monsters and chimeras. Mermaids and centaurs exist only in myths.

We are concerned with sex and the energies involved in sexual phenomena. We have landed in the mazes of molecular biology in which vast and incredibly complex molecules writhe like serpents, unzipper and reconstitute themselves in a submicroscopic frenzy of activity with consequences that are momentous at the level of the organism. (One error can spell cancer, degeneracy, death.) All phenomena at the level of the organism are manifestations of the molecular dance associated with the separation and reblending of vital codes. In the focus of our awareness is the chromosome, a complex though micro-scopic object. Forty-six of them inhabit every cell in our body with the exception of our sperm cells if we happen to be male and our egg cells if we happen to be female. They pass through an orderly cycle, shorten and thicken, marshal themselves in the center of the cell, are drawn to the opposite poles as the cell divides, forty-six to one side, forty-six to the other. Before the cell divides they have divided, splitting along the middle of the molecular code, reconstituting the code, just as it was before. The two cells which result from cellular division each receives a perfect copy of the DNA code and proceeds on the basis of instructions in that code to go about its biochemical business, which is the formation of protein, the stuff of life.

A complete copy of the code goes to every cell in the body with one exception. This exception is the sex cell (Fig. 4). In

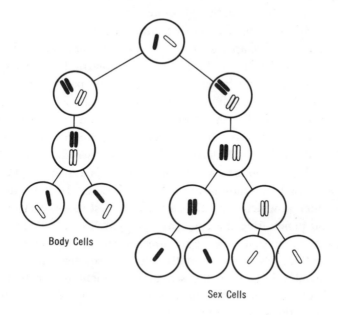

Body Cells

Sex Cells

4. Division of the genetic code. Body cells receive a double set of chromosomes, sex cells a single set.

the formation of sex cells we encounter a new mechanism, a special form of cell division. For it must be obvious to the thoughtful that, if cells are to unite and still keep the same number of chromosomes they must undergo, at some time, a *reduction* in chromosome number. If the body cell has 2x chromosome then the sex cell must contain x.

Here is the ultimate secret of micro-sex. The genetic code, double in the body cell, is halved in the sex cell by a mechanism that remains a mystery to the scientist. Why, out of all the billions of cells in the body, do these *gametes* or "marrying cells" divide by an entirely different mechanism? The chromosomes parade in the equator of the sex cell but they do not split down the middle and reconstitute the missing halves. Instead, each member of a chromosome pair goes off in an opposite direction. In man the two cells which result from this "reduction division" contain twenty-three chromosomes each. Twenty-two are "somatic" chromosomes (autosomes), one is a "sex" chromosome. The two sex chromosomes are quite different in size and shape, a large "X" chromosome, a small "Y" chromosome. In the X chromosomes are carried the parts of the code that confer femaleness, in the Y the parts that confer maleness. All normal human females contain two X chromosomes in their bodies. All normal eggs contain one X chromosome. But the male is a hybrid creature with one X and one Y in his body cells, the X derived from his mother, the Y from his father (Fig. 5). So his sex cells or sperm cells are equally likely to carry an X chromosome or a Y chromosome. In the cellular marathon on which our fates depend the first sperm cell reaching and penetrating the egg may carry an X or a Y. When an X carrier penetrates the egg there results an XX being who, if everything else goes normally, will emerge from the womb nine months later with the sexual equipment of the female. If a Y carrier penetrates the egg the resulting XY individual will carry the sexual equipment of the male.

XX versus XY—the ultimate difference. It enters into every

cell in the body. It affects everything, muscular strength, distribution of fat, distribution of body hair, proportions of the limbs, patterns of movement, even patterns of thought. There are those who believe that the double X of the female makes her the more richly endowed of the two sexes. For the Y, at least in man, is a poor shrunken thing, little better than a dummy, and seems to carry little genetic information. The X, by contrast, is one of the larger chromosomes. In some respects the female is better endowed. She is more durable. Her life expectancy, in the United States, is now 73.9 years as compared with the male's 67.3 years. But if the possession of an extra X were the secret of superior biological vigor then surely the possession of three X should produce a superman (or superwoman). There are such people. The reduction division that forms the egg does not always work perfectly and an egg containing two X chromosomes sometimes results. When such

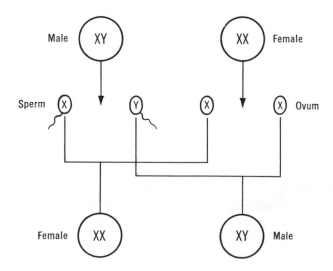

5. *Distribution of the sex chromosomes:*
XX versus XY makes the ultimate difference.

an egg is fertilized by an X-carrying cell there results an XXX being. Similarly when the reduction division of the sperm breaks down, a sperm may carry both X and Y, giving rise after fertilization to a being having XXY.

But this extra genetic material does not confer any advantages on its possessor. The XXX, far from being a super-female, is generally poorly developed, mentally defective. The XXY is also defective. Research has even brought to light an individual with the extraordinary collection of four X chromosomes and one Y. The result was an imbecile with an I.Q. of 21, a cleft palate, cross-eyed, with an exceptionally small penis and atrophied testicles. Nor does an extra Y chromosome seem to offer any blessings, though individuals possessing it have been termed super-males in some reports. The only thing super about such people is that they tend to be over six feet tall. They commonly have low I.Q.'s, are excessively aggressive, prone to crime and commonly end up in prison. An excess of sex chromosomes does not confer super sex.

CELLULAR MARRIAGE

Because our lives and fates depend on them it is worth our while to study with some care the formation of the sex cells within our bodies. Careless, prodigal nature forms these entities in such numbers that the biosphere is permanently awash in a sea of sperm. She is somewhat less lavish with the eggs, but there is little danger of a shortage.

Sperm formation in man takes place in the testicles. These paired glands dangle outside of the body in a hairy sac which gives them an environment 2°C. cooler than that enjoyed by other organs of the body. Coolness seems necessary. An overheated testicle is a sterile testicle. Hundreds of little coiled tubes, like a knotted mass of worms, make up the bulk of the testicle. During the first ten years of life these tubes lie inactive but as puberty approaches they start to grow. A signal from the master gland at the base of the brain (pituitary) awakens them into a frenzy of activity and the astonished adolescent (fourteen to fifteen years old) finds himself not only a prey to unusual desires but also a generator of a strange whitish fluid, a part of which is produced by the furiously proliferating tubes. This proliferation takes a unique form. In the wall of the tube special cells called *spermatogonia* divide to give two *spermatocytes* from which arise four *spermatids* (Fig. 6). These spermatids, having only half the usual number of chromosomes, are then transformed without further cell division into some of the most peculiar cells of the body, the *spermatozoa*.

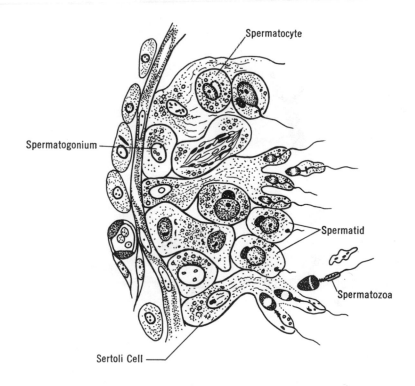

6. *Formation of spermatozoa, the male sex cells.*

Spermatozoa are produced in incredible numbers. At any one time the tubes in the testicle (which would measure about twenty-seven inches if laid end to end) produce 300 million sperm, only one of which is needed to fertilize the egg. The creatures are tiny. Enough to generate the entire population of a continent could be piled on the head of a pin. They are completely unlike any other cell in the body, having a head, a neck, a middle piece and a tail, which gives them the aspect of an elongated tadpole (Fig. 7). The important part of the tiny beast is contained in the head, which measures only 0.0046 × 0.0026 mm. Into this minute space is packed an entire genetic code representing the paternal half of inheritance.

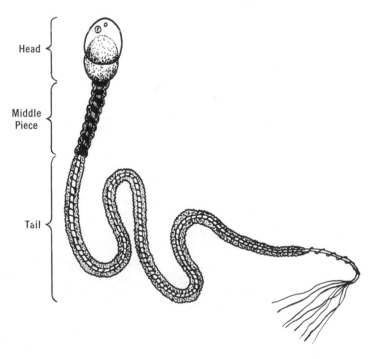

Head

Middle Piece

Tail

7. *Detailed structure of spermatozoon. Enough of them to generate the population of a continent could be piled on the head of a pin.*

The rest of the animal is only concerned with swimming and appears to carry no information whatever.

The spermatozoa are produced continuously. They are moved from the tubes in the testicles and stored in a small sac (the seminal vesicle) between the urinary bladder and the rectum. At the climax of the sexual act this sac contracts vigorously, expelling the sperm which are mixed with products of other glands and emerge in a series of jets from the urethra, a passage which, such is nature's unromantic economy, they share with the urine.

The spermatozoa swim in the fluid in which they are ejected, a soupy brew derived from prostate, seminal ducts (*vasa deferentia*), seminal vesicles, Cowper's glands and other glands (Fig. 20). The whole mixture is semen. Semen can be divided into two parts, the seminal plasma in which the spermatozoa swim and the spermatozoa themselves. It is ejected in a definite order. In man the secretion of Cowper's glands is ejected first, the prostatic secretion next, followed by sperm and the product of the seminal vesicles. The prostate, a gland that often proves more of a curse than a blessing to its possessor because of its tendency to turn cancerous, contributes up to 30 percent of the semen. The seminal vesicles may contribute up to 80 percent. The spermatozoa may be only 10 percent of the total ejaculate. Volume of semen varies from one animal to another and from one male to another. In man it ranges from 2 to 10 milliliters (a thimbleful). In the boar it may reach 500 milliliters (a generous cupful). Frequency of ejaculation is dependent on age and sexual vigor. The bull, when given no choice in the matter (a simple electrical device inserted in the rectum promotes the discharge whenever the current is applied), ejaculated eight times in a little over an hour. Under these conditions the volume of semen fell from 4.2 to 2.9 ml. and the sperm density per milliliter from 1,644,000 to 98,000. Total semen ejaculated was 28 ml. The bull is noted for its semen-producing capacity. It is doubtful if any man could equal this performance.

Spermatozoa, once ejaculated into the female body, encounter an environment that is not friendly to their survival. It is too hot and too acid. They would die almost at once were the seminal plasma absent, but the latter is buffered, as chemists say, and prevents the acidity of the vagina from killing the spermatozoa. Even so they live for a short while only. At the climax of coition about 300 million of them are forcibly ejected against the mouth of the womb. (This is the situation in man. In the pig they are injected into the womb itself.) The cervix (mouth of the womb) is closed by a plug of mucus but the spermatozoa are able to penetrate this barrier (bacteria swarming in the vagina lack this capacity). Pouring through the cervix into the uterus the invading sperm-swarm swims furiously. Though guided neither by sight nor smell they tend to swim against the current (in the uterus this current flows downward and outward). The tiny voyagers have a trip ahead of them which, in proportion to their length, is long and dangerous. If deposited against the mouth of the womb they must swim through the uterus (7 cm.) and along most of the uterine tube (10 to 12 cm.). (See Fig. 8.) So they must cover 4,000 times their own length, a journey equivalent, for a man, to swimming nearly five miles.

Few of those who set out complete the voyage. Of the hundreds of millions ejaculated only a few thousand reach the end of the tube and only one actually fertilizes the egg. During the trip the sperm undergo a subtle change known as capacitation which renders them capable of penetrating the egg surface. The nature of this change is not understood. Spermatozoa survive in the female tract for a short time only. In such mammals as man they live from twenty-four to forty-eight hours, though in the bat they survive for months. As the male-producing sperm is slightly lighter than the female-producing sperm it may have an edge in the great race. This may explain the slight preponderance of male births over female (106:100).

The second partner of cellular marriage, the egg cell or ovum, is formed by a very different process from that which gives rise to the sperm. Eggs are formed in the ovaries, the female equivalent of the testicles. Unlike the latter, these ovaries are embedded in the body cavity, for the full warmth of the body seems not to affect the egg as it does the sperm. The two ovaries lie on either side of the pelvis, are white oval bodies about one and a half inches long and half an inch thick. They are not made up of tubes like the testicles, but consist instead of clusters of cells called follicle cells (Fig. 8). In the center of each cluster is a larger cell called an *oogonium*. This is the egg cell of the future.

When a girl baby is born her ovaries may contain as many as 300,000 oogonia, a trifling sum compared with the untold billions of spermatozoa generated in the body of the male during sexual life, but more than adequate for reproductive

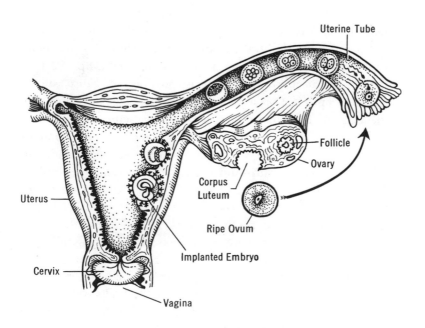

8. *Ripening of the ovum and implantation of early embryo. "Thus is human life launched into the inner space."*

purposes. The ovaries remain dormant until the signal comes from the pituitary which indicates that puberty is on the way. By this time many of the oogonia have died and only about 15,000 remain. Of these only about 200 will ever ripen.

The ripening process which gives rise to the egg occurs throughout the reproductive life of the normal woman. Her whole existence may be dominated by its rhythm, for nature's peculiar arrangements are such, in the human at least, that no female can remain unaware of this inner cycle. The egg cells mature and are discharged from the surface of the ovary at intervals of twenty-eight to thirty days during a span which may extend from the eleventh to the forty-fifth year of the woman's life. The egg is discharged most often fourteen days after the onset of menstruation, but may emerge as early as eight days or as late as twenty days after this date.

Discharge of the egg is the final stage of the process of egg maturation. Unlike the male, whose testicles manufacture sperm cells by the billion, the female (human) normally produces only one egg from her ovaries a month. Special hormones control the process. It is possible to cause superovulation (production of as many as thirty eggs at a time) by injections of these hormones, a fact now being made use of by livestock breeders. But for most women one egg a month is quite enough to worry about. When the egg cell begins to enlarge it becomes surrounded by a transparent layer called the *zona pellucida,* a sort of capsule which encloses the egg like an eggshell. Outside the capsule a layer of special cells forms and grows progressively thicker. These are the nurse cells that feed the growing egg, 3,000 to 4,000 cells all connected together like tributaries of a stream pouring their contents into the egg. The egg grows rapidly and attains a size that makes it one of the largest cells of the body. When fully grown it is 0.176 mm. across (with the *zona pellucida*), 90,000 times the size of the spermatozoon.

As the egg enlarges, the follicle in the ovary enlarges also. It began life as a dense mass of granular cells with an egg in the middle. Soon it becomes hollow and before long attains the form of a hollow sphere 10 mm. across. When fully developed the follicle lies under the surface of the ovary and is filled with fluid. The fluid increases in amount, generating pressure. Suddenly the follicle bursts and its liquid contents, including the egg, are poured into the abdominal cavity. Oddly enough there is no direct connection between the ovary and the opening of the uterine tube, nothing in fact to prevent the egg from being lost in the relatively vast spaces of the abdominal cavity. Now and then an egg does get lost in this way. Normally the egg is swept into the tube by the action of myriad hairlike cilia that generate a current downward and outward and keep the egg rolling in the direction of the uterus.

Now the egg is ready for cellular marriage. It underwent, just before being liberated from the follicle, that all-important division which reduced the number of its chromosomes from forty-six to twenty-three. The result of this division was not two eggs but one egg and a spare nucleus, a mere by-product, extruded into the space under the *zona pellucida* and known as a polar body. This generally divides again to form two polar bodies.

At this stage the egg lies in the upper reaches of the uterine tube. If it has arrived at this point about twenty-four hours after coitus it will encounter a swarm of capacitated spermatozoa. There is no evidence that the egg cell attracts the sperm. They may swarm right past the egg, in close proximity, without so much as a swerve in its direction. Contact seems accidental at this micro-sexual level, but having once accidentally touched the egg the vast majority of sperm remain attached. The accumulation of this cloud of sperm gives the ovum a fuzzy appearance as if it had sprouted hair (Fig. 9). Although the ovum is 90,000 times bigger than they are, the clinging sperm are so numerous and move their tails so vigorously that they set the egg rolling. It rotates, Dr. L. B. Shettles informs us, once in fifteen minutes, always clockwise, for as long as twenty to thirty hours.[1]

All this occurs when the egg is less than two hours old. In fact, if a new human being is to result from the frenzy of cellular activity, the egg cannot be much older than this. Two hours is about the limit of the life of the human egg.

Of the thousands of spermatozoa that surround the egg a few penetrate through the *zona pellucida,* that clear envelope that surrounds the egg like an eggshell. As soon as penetration occurs the nucleus of the egg divides again, expelling one nucleus as a polar body. The egg thus has three polar bodies under the *zona pellucida.* They contain just as much of the genetic code as the egg cell itself, but they have no cytoplasm. Now and then, according to Dr. Shettles, polar bodies may be fertilized, producing fraternal twins of markedly different birth weights.

Penetration of the egg by the sperm is not the most vital

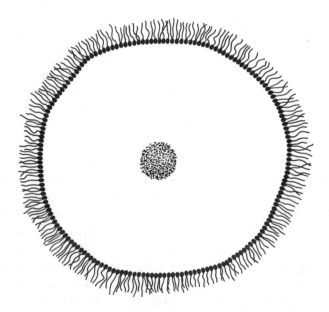

9. *Ovum surrounded by sperm. The cloud of sperm gives the ovum a fuzzy appearance.*

part of cellular marriage because penetration is not the same as fertilization. The human egg may be penetrated by several sperm. (Other eggs, those of the starfish for instance, produce a fertilization membrane as soon as a sperm has penetrated the egg which prevents the entrance of other sperm.) For fertilization to occur the sperm must burrow deeply into the substance of the egg. It does this, tail and all, and comes to rest close to the nucleus of the egg cell. Here the sperm loses its characteristic form. The tail disappears. The head becomes a spherical nucleus of the same size as the female nucleus. It is only at this point, in an obscurity so profound as to be out of reach of any but the most patient microscopist, that the cellular marriage is finally consummated. The two nuclei, one from the male and the other from the female, touch and fuse, producing a single nucleus in which the double number of chromosomes characteristic of body cells is restored. The result of the cellular marriage is the *zygote* which proceeds to divide into two cells, four cells, eight cells, a ball of cells, a hollow sphere of cells which goes rolling down the Fallopian tubes to embed itself like a leech in the juicy lining of the uterus. Thus, as Dr. Shettles puts it, is human life launched into the inner space.

**II.
VARIETIES
OF SEXUAL
UNION**

A SCALE OF SEX ENERGY

MICRO SEX RESULTS in cellular marriage, the union of a moving active sperm cell with a large immobile egg cell. The genetic code is reshuffled. A new being results similar to but not identical with the two beings who produced it. Sperm are produced in the body of the male and the egg in the body of the female. The closer these bodies can come to each other the greater will be the chance of egg and sperm uniting.

Sex energy can best be defined as the force that operates to bring these male and female bodies together. This energy is manifested in various ways and at many different levels of life. It is necessary now that we review these manifestations.

We begin with a scale of sex energy. At the bottom of the scale are the weakest possible manifestations of this force. Among oysters, starfish, jellyfish, even among fairly complex forms such as the lancet and several true fish, there is absolutely no attractive force acting to bring male and female together. Sperm and eggs are shed into the ocean and meet only because they are produced in enormous numbers. Plants, lacking the capacity for motion, cannot be said to manifest sex energy at all. Some plants such as maize rely on the wind and must produce huge quantities of pollen to ensure that the feathery stigmas of the female flowers are pollinated. Plants that rely on insects to transport pollen from one flower to another can hardly be said to manifest sex energy through this strange mechanism. Insect pollination is an oddity of evolution and does not belong on the scale of sex energy at all.

33

Above the oysters and starfish we can place such forms as the newt. Newts do not copulate. They do not even embrace. Nonetheless the male is attracted to the female, dances in front of her, lays a packet of sperm at her feet. A slightly stronger force operates between leeches in which the male places his spermatophore on the female body. Fish are drawn together in pairs by complex forces, involving patterns of behavior that seem strange to the mammalian observer. Actual copulation does not take place though fertilization is internal in such forms as the dogfish. Frogs unite firmly and for long periods but true copulation does not occur because the male has no penis.

Copulation proper occurs among insects, reptiles and mammals so that these forms, diverse as they are, may be placed in a single category as far as sex energy is concerned. But the forces that draw male and female together are extremely varied. Among insects chemical attractants (pheromones) play a special role. The mammals are for the most part bound by cyclic fluctuations in hormone production which ensure that the male is drawn to the female only at certain times of the year. Man, dominated by his brain rather than his hormones, falls into a special category. Male and female may unite at any time and are more or less permanently attracted. By the standards of other mammals man is excessively, almost insanely sexual. His cousins the apes and monkeys are very restrained by comparison.

Man probably represents the form in which sex energy works most often and perhaps most strongly. For sheer richness of sexual experience the highest place must be awarded to such copulating hermaphrodites as the snail. Accordingly these have been placed in a special category. They are sexually the most abundantly endowed of living creatures and their hermaphrodite copulatory orgies with sado-masochistic overtones make any human excesses seem comparatively dull. We will now consider in more detail these varied manifestations of sex energy.

SEED CAST ON WIND OR WATER

Oysters are not ardent lovers. They lead an uncomplicated existence anchored to a rock, filtering their food out of the seawater, which they strain by ceaseless rhythmic movements of hairlike cells on their gills. There is not the slightest visible difference between a female oyster and a male oyster; in fact, like a number of other mollusks, the same oyster can be both. Not, however, at the same time. The European flat oyster enjoys the best of both worlds by being a male one year and a female the next. This oyster is slightly less careless in its reproductive habits than its relative, the American oyster. It sheds its sperm (when in the male phase) at random into the sea but it holds onto its eggs (when in the female phase) by depositing them on its gills. Sperm are drawn in along with other particles in the ceaseless stream of water that passes over the gills, but for some reason the sperm are able to avoid being eaten and fertilize the eggs instead. The American oyster abandons even this economy, sheds its eggs, along with sperm, into the sea. It needs, for this reason, to produce large numbers of eggs to ensure reproduction. Careless though it is, the oyster does at least have a habit of casting eggs and sperm into the sea at the same time. Were it not for this mechanism the creature must surely long ago have become extinct.

Many other marine animals, plus most of the marine plants (seaweeds), share the American oyster's casual method of mating. Sea anemones, sea urchins, starfish, all tend to reproduce by casting their eggs and sperm into the sea. Some of the starfish have developed the pattern of brood care characteristic of the European oyster. They produce relatively small numbers of yolk-rich eggs which they hold in brood pouches or pockets between their spines. There is no meeting between male and female starfish even in these forms. The sperm are shed into the sea in enormous numbers and their encounter with the eggs depends on the movement of the water.

There are land plants also that cast their sperm into the water, though the water in this case is rarely more than a film of dew on the underside of a frond. The fern, to the unobservant, is a showy plant inhabiting damp places and reproducing by spores that are borne on the leaves. But the fern has a secret sex life that few observe, for its spores produce an insignificant plantlet entirely made up of haploid cells (half the full number of chromosomes). This insignificant film of vegetation has on its under surface both male and female organs. The male organs shed their swimming sperm into a film of dew in which they proceed to the neck of the female organ, attracted by a chemical substance called malic acid. They swim in and unite with the female nucleus and from the zygote so formed a new (diploid) fern arises which produces spores as before.

Here there is no meeting of male and female because male and female organs are borne on the same plant and the fern thus generally succeeds in fertilizing itself. A somewhat similar mechanism exists in the violet which bears, in addition to the fragrant flowers for which it is famed, small secret blooms called cleistogamic flowers that regularly fertilize themselves, committing a sort of botanical incest.

The violet might better have been chosen as a symbol of hypocrisy than of modesty.

INSECT INTERMEDIARIES

The flowering plants may bear male and female flowers on different plants or the flower may have both male parts and female parts (stamens which produce pollen and stigmas to catch the pollen). In either case the pollen (equivalent to the sperm of the animal) must be transferred to the stigma of a different plant if sexual reproduction is to produce any reblending of genetic codes. Wind pollination is chancy and involves the production of vast amounts of pollen. So some plants have developed one of the strangest of all biological mechanisms, pollination by insects.

Familiarity with this mechanism prevents us from regarding it with the astonishment it deserves. If human lovers were unable to move and if the male developed a habit of entrusting his sperm to the care of some bee or beetle which would deposit them in the vagina of the female in exchange for a drink of sugar water we would have an approximate picture of the strangeness of this behavior pattern. But only approximate. For the flower is a device of such complexity and adapts itself to the form of the insect pollinator so elegantly that no meaningful analogy is possible. Fantastic structures, as complex as they are decorative, abound in the plant world. They are designed to ensure that the visiting insect deposits pollen on the female organ of another flower rather than fertilizing the flower with its own pollen.

These mechanisms reach their ultimate complexity among members of the orchid family. The pollen is collected in sticky sacs, glued to the head of the visiting insects, then passed to the receptive female of another flower by the complex acrobatics imposed on the insects by the structure of the flower. Bribes used by the flowers range from the fecal or carrionlike stench emitted by certain arums, which is attractive to flies, all the way to the most ethereal and elegant perfumes which, combined with a sip of sugar water, entice the bee, most versatile and industrious of all pollinators.

DEVOURING LOVE

No member of the animal kingdom employs an insect intermediary for the purpose of bringing together sperm and egg. There are, however, many devices used for this purpose by animals that must strike us as curious if not downright repulsive. The bloodsucking leech, for example, is an unlovable creature at best and its sexual habits are as unattractive as its feeding habits. Leeches are hermaphrodites, which means that the same individual produces both eggs and sperm. They have, however, neither of the organs traditionally associated with the performance of the sexual act, being devoid both of a penis for introducing sperm and of a vagina for receiving the same. When leeches mate, the one that plays the role of the male clings to the body of the one that plays the female. While thus clinging it deposits on its partner's body a sac-shaped capsule called a spermatophore. The capsule contains sperm under pressure and produces from its attached end a powerful, flesh-dissolving enzyme that eats a hole through the body wall of the female. Through this hole the sperm are injected forcibly into the female's body cavity. Once in the cavity the sperm are attacked by special cells which eat them. Those that survive may be carried by the body fluid to the ovaries where they may pass through the walls and fertilize the eggs inside. The leech in the female role is left with a gaping flesh wound that takes three days to repair.

Another technique which might have tickled the fancy of the Marquis de Sade is used by the sea worm, *Platynereis megalops*. These worms swarm together at spawning time and, when the number of males and females has reached the density necessary for an orgy, the females attack the males, bite off their tails and swallow them; a love feast in the most literal sense of the term! The males, like most worms, have well-developed powers of regeneration. They swim away and grow new segments. The females digest their cannibalistic feast which happens to contain the male's testes and his entire supply of sperm. The spermatozoa, liberated by the female's digestive juices, penetrate the wall of the gut, find their way into her body cavity, locate and fertilize her eggs. This passage through the female digestive tract, hazardous though it may seem, is necessary to activate the sperm. Spermatozoa that have not passed through this ordeal are incapable of fertilizing the egg.

The palolo worm of Samoa and the Fiji Islands manages its

sex life somewhat differently. Adult worms living in crevices in the coral reefs produce from their tails chains of segments, each a worm in itself, loaded with eggs or with sperm. The segments break off and swim in huge numbers to the surface of the sea. There they burst, releasing eggs and sperm into the water. The spent worm fragments sink to the bottom and die.

The palolo worm's reproductive orgy takes place in November, one week after the full moon. So precise is its timing that the natives of Samoa celebrate all night in anticipation of the worm feast. In the first gray light of dawn they put to sea, gathering the sexual worm segments by the thousand in baskets, for they regard them as the greatest of delicacies. Safe in their coral crevices the adult worms regenerate their missing tails, preparing for another orgy in November of the following year.

Peripatus, a strange animal that occupies a niche somewhere between the worms and the insects, imitates the leech in its habit of laying a spermatophore on its mate's back, which then eats a hole in the flesh through which the sperm enter. Other varieties of this beast engage in the practice of fertilization by hypodermic injection. The male's reproductive tract ends in a sharp spine. He drives this right through the female's skin and places the sperm in the depth of her body cavity.

The bedbug, another bloodsucker, comes together with its mate in a manner that might be considered conventional, for the male has a penis and the female a vagina and it would seem necessary only for the eager pair to employ these organs in the traditional way for all the needs of love to be satisfied. Not so. The bedbug's penis is a warped, large, inflexible, lopsided structure that cannot possibly fit into the female genital opening. So instead of mating in the normal way the bedbug injects its sperm into a special sac on the right side of the female's body. As this sac has no connection with the oviducts or ovaries the sperm can only enter the female by passing between the cells that line the sac and traveling up the walls of the female reproductive tract. Their journey is perilous, for the bedbug, like the leech, has developed special cells that devour the sperm. Nonetheless, in spite of all these handicaps, the bedbug has survived to plague the human race.

In all these forms the force that draws the male and female together is difficult to evaluate. The fruits of love seem strange and unappetizing. The leech receives holes in its flesh. The male *Platynereis* has its tail bitten off. The female *Peripatus* has a dagger driven into her vitals. The copulatory thrill, which nature dangles as a bait before men and women to induce them to continue that routine rhythm without which the race would vanish, is nowhere in evidence.

The sex life of spiders would seem even more unrewarding; indeed it is beset with such hazards that it seems a miracle that these creatures have survived. Far from feeling any urge to embrace his mate, the male spider has every reason to stay as far from her as possible, it being her practice, when the rites of Venus have been completed, to refresh herself by dining off her husband. So the male quite literally keeps the female at arm's length by utilizing for sexual purposes not an intimate penis but a remote organ called a palp, at the end of one of his four pairs of legs. As this palp has no direct connection with the sperm-producing glands, the spider uses an indirect method of transferring its semen (Fig. 10). First it spins a special web, then deposits on the web a drop of semen, dips each palp into the semen, thereby filling a little organ like a small hypodermic syringe called the *receptaculum seminalis*. One of these syringes he inserts into the genital orifice of the female, shoots in the semen, then scuttles off as fast as possible to avoid his mate's embrace and the prospect of being turned into a quick snack.

The cannibalistic tendencies of the female spider have been developed even further among the insects. That sensitive and accurate observer of insect life, Jean Henri Fabre, was shocked by such deviations of the sexual impulse. "What shall we say,"

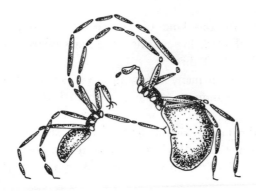

10. Mating of spiders. The male keeps the female at a safe distance by mating with one of its legs.

he asks, "when the saddle grasshopper, before laying her eggs, slits her mate open and eats as much of him as she can hold? And when the gentle cricket becomes a hyena and mercilessly pulls out the wings of her beloved, who performed so magnificent a serenade for her, smashes his harp and shows her thanks by partially devouring him?" [2]

An even more gruesome performance is staged by the golden ground beetle whose feats of nuptial cannibalism were described by Fabre as follows: "A vain struggle to break away—that is all the male undertakes toward his salvation. Otherwise, he accepts his fate. Finally his skin bursts, the wound gapes wide, the inner substance is devoured by his worthy spouse. Her head burrowing inside the body of her husband, she hollows out his back. A shudder that runs through the poor fellow's limbs announces his approaching end. The female butcher ignores this; she gropes into the narrowest passages and windings in the thoracic cavity. Soon only the well-known little boat of the wing sheaths and the thorax with legs attached are left of the dead male. The husk, sucked dry, is abandoned."

The prize for this kind of love feast would probably be awarded to the praying mantis (Fig. 11) whose habits were also described by Fabre.

"The Mantis, in many cases, is never sated with conjugal raptures and banquets. After a rest that varies in length, whether the eggs be laid or not, a second male is accepted and then devoured like the first. A third succeeds him, performs his function in life, is eaten and disappears. A fourth undergoes a like fate. In the course of two weeks I thus see

11. Male and female mantises. During mating the male becomes a banquet for his spouse.

one and the same Mantis use up seven males. She takes them all to her bosom and makes them all pay for the nuptial ecstasy with their lives. I find, by themselves, a horrible couple engaged as follows. The male, absorbed in the performance of his vital functions, holds the female in a tight embrace. But the wretch has no head; he has no neck; he has hardly a body. The other, with her muzzle turned over her shoulder, continues very placidly to gnaw what remains of the gentle swain. And, all the time, that masculine stump, holding on firmly, goes on with the business!

"Love is stronger than death men say. Taken literally, the aphorism has never received a more brilliant confirmation. A headless creature, an insect amputated down to the middle of the chest, a very corpse, persists in endeavoring to give life. It will not let go until the abdomen, the seat of the procreative organs is attacked."

These findings saddened Fabre. "I have seen it done with my own eyes," he wrote, "and have not recovered from my astonishment." They would probably have delighted another Frenchman, one who never wearied of emphasizing the essential criminality of nature: "Oh, rest assured, no crime in the world is capable of drawing the wrath of Nature upon us; all crimes serve her purpose, all are useful to her, and when she inspires us do not doubt but that she has need of them" (De Sade, *Juliette*).

LOVE FACTORY

Those prone to "view with alarm" the course of human affairs often deplore the increasing mechanization of life. Man is becoming a slave to his machines. He is himself becoming a machine. Individuality is being sacrificed. Mass conformity is the rule. We are following the road to the anthill or the road to the termitary.

Such lamentations may also include a reference to the regimented sex life of the social insects and involve somber warnings that human sex life may become similarly regimented. All of which gives us reason to explore the rather peculiar manifestations of sex energy that have developed among these forms.

We begin with the honeybees, *Apis mellifera*. Here we confront a situation in which sexual activity has been eliminated from the lives of almost all the members of the colony. Within the beehive copulation is unknown. The thousands of workers who come and go incessantly bearing pollen or nectar from the flowers they have visited are all females. They are, however, merely genetically female, for their sex organs are not formed and they cannot mate. These female workers are all produced from a fertilized egg and have the usual double number of chromosomes. There are also males in the hive, the so-called drones, who do no work and exist only to fertilize the queen. These males are produced from unfertilized eggs and are peculiar in having only half the number of chromosomes of the workers. The sperm cells of the male bee are not produced by that reducing division which, in other animals, serves to ensure that these cells receive only half the number to begin with. Its sex cells contain the same number of chromosomes as its body cells.

Sex energy among the bees is manifested only once during the life of the queen. It does this in a manner so dramatic as to evoke the astonishment of scientists and the admiration of poets. Maeterlinck, writing before the Great Disenchantment made writers wary of rapture, devoted several pages of purple prose to describing the event.

"She soars to a height, a luminous zone, that other bees attain at no period of their life. Far away, caressing their idleness in the midst of the flowers, the males have beheld the apparition, have breathed the magnetic perfume that spreads from group to group till every apiary near is instinct with it.

Immediately crowds collect, and follow her into the sea of gladness, whose limpid boundaries ever recede. She, drunk with her wings, obeying the magnificent law of the race that chooses her lover, and enacts that the strongest alone shall attain her in the solitude of the ether, she rises still; and, for the first time in her life, the blue morning air rushes into her stigmata, singing its song, like the blood of heaven, in the myriad tubes of the tracheal sacs, nourished on space, that fill the center of her body. She rises still. A region must be found unhaunted by birds, that else might profane the mystery. She rises still; and already the ill-assorted troop below are dwindling and falling asunder. The feeble, infirm, the aged, unwelcome, ill-fed, who have flown from inactive or impoverished cities, these renounce the pursuit and disappear in the void. Only a small, indefatigable cluster remain, suspended in infinite opal. She summons her wings for one final effort; and now the chosen of incomprehensible forces has reached her, has seized her, and bounding aloft with united impetus, the ascending spiral of their intertwined flight whirls for one second in the hostile madness of love." [3]

The "hostile madness," in this instance, refers to the fact that the female bee kills her mate not by devouring him, as does the praying mantis, but by tearing out of his abdomen his entire genital apparatus. The gutted Romeo falls to earth. The queen "descends from the azure heights and returns to the hive, trailing, like an oriflamme, the unfolded entrails of her lover." His death is of no importance. She has taken from him the only thing that counts and has stored in her spermatheca his entire stock of sperm, enough to enable her to lay fertile eggs at the rate of two thousand a day for as long as five years. Some quite unfathomable instinct in the queen enables her to control the sex of the beings she produces. A tiny squeeze of the spermatheca will eject enough sperm to fertilize the passing egg and the resulting bee will be female. No squeeze, no fertilization and the resulting bee will be a male (drone). Thus the queen has power to control the sex of her offspring (a capacity human mothers may envy) as long as her store of sperm lasts. When it runs out she will lay eggs that produce nothing but drones, a condition known to beekeepers as drone broodiness.

Worker bees, technically female, are functionally neuter. They have neither sexual impulses nor sex organs. Their entire existence is geared to the needs of the community. They care for the young, feed and clean the queen, collect pollen or nectar, make cells for the storage of honey, and brood cells in three different sizes for workers, drones or queens.

It may be asked why all workers do not become queens. The answer is curious and indicates how intimately sexual development may be associated with diet. There is a food secreted by special glands of the worker bee which beekeepers call royal jelly. All workers are fed on this substance for the first three days of life but those destined to become queens (from eggs placed in special large brood cells) are fed on royal jelly continuously and hatch sixteen days later as young queens. The first young queen to emerge murders all her sister queens promptly and instinctively by stinging them before they have even emerged from their brood cells. She then proceeds to the mystical flight as described.

Nobody knows why royal jelly exerts this dramatic effect on the sexual development of the bee. The substance is rich in vitamins and various hormones. From time to time manufacturers of cosmetics promote creams containing royal jelly, suggesting that a substance that makes a fertile queen bee from a sterile worker bee ought to do wonders for human females also. It is a nice thought.

Murder of rival queens is only one of the massacres that routinely occur in the beehive. More spectacular is the murder of the drones, the surplus males, who are periodically set upon by the workers, "an army of wrathful virgins" as Maeterlinck called them, and exterminated. As an example of sentimen-

talizing and anthropomorphizing the Belgian poet's description
of this event is hard to equal; it does, however, emphasize the
prevalence of violence and cruelty in nature and one cannot
help wondering whether the force that compels the sterile females to murder the drones is a distorted form of sex energy.

"Each one is assailed by three or four envoys of justice; and
these vigorously proceed to cut off his wings, saw through the
petiole that connects the abdomen with the thorax, amputate
the feverish antennae, and seek an opening between the rings
of his cuirass through which to pass their sword. No defense
is attempted by the enormous, but unarmed, creatures; they
try to escape, or oppose their mere bulk to the blows that rain
down upon them. Forced on to their back, with their relent-
less enemies clinging doggedly to them, they will use their
powerful claws to shift them from side to side; or, turning on
themselves, they will drag the whole group round and round
in wild circles, which exhaustion soon brings to an end. And,
in a very brief space, their appearance becomes so deplorable
that pity, never far from justice in the depths of our heart,
quickly returns, and would seek forgiveness, though vainly,
of the stern workers who recognize only nature's harsh and
profound laws. The wings of the wretched creatures are torn,
their antennae bitten, the segments of their legs wrenched off,
and their magnificent eyes, mirrors once of the exuberant
flowers, flashing back the blue light and the innocent pride of
summer, now, softened by suffering, reflect only the anguish
and distress of their end. Some succumb to their wounds, and
are at once borne away to distant cemeteries by two or three
of their executioners. Others, whose injuries are less, succeed
in sheltering themselves in some corner where they lie, all
huddled together, surrounded by an inexorable guard, until
they perish of want. Many will reach the door, and escape into
space, dragging their adversaries with them; but, toward evening, impelled by hunger and cold, they return in crowds to
the entrance of the hive to beg for shelter. But there they en-

counter another pitiless guard. The next morning, before setting forth on their journey, the workers will clear the threshold, strewn with the corpses of the useless giants; and all recollection of the idle race disappears till the following spring." [3]

Quite a different relationship between the sexes exists among the termites. These insects, though commonly called white ants, are not ants at all but are related to cockroaches. This relationship would place the termites in one of the most primitive group of insects as far as the evolutionary scale is concerned. There is, however, nothing primitive about their social organization which has been defined by Karl Escherich as "the culmination of animal social life." So extraordinary is their society that both Maurice Maeterlinck and Eugene Marais felt compelled to postulate the existence of some "occult power" or "soul" that integrated the behavior of these insects. Marais even went so far as to suggest that the termitary is "a single composite animal at a specific stage of development." [4] He compared the hard clay shell of the termite mound with the skin, the corridors with arteries, workers with blood cells, the royal chamber with the heart, brain and reproductive apparatus of the composite organism.

Sex in the termitary is nonexistent both for the workers and for the soldiers. These can be technically either male or female but the sex organs are not functional and their possessors are too busy to care about sex. There are, however, "innumerable legions of youths and maidens with long transparent wings and faceted eyes . . . In them are centered the hopes, the dreams of luxury and voluptuous joy, of a sepulchral city, that has no other avenue to the sky or to love." [5]

These winged forms wander idly through the corridors of the termitary, fed by the workers with predigested food, for, lacking the protozoa in their intestines that digest the woody particles on which termites feed, these forms must always eat at second hand. When the rainy season brings the tropical summer to an end these winged forms emerge from the termitaries in swarms so vast that they arouse astonishment even in those dwellers in the tropics who have regularly witnessed the event. "From an area of hundreds of acres, there rises, as from an overcharged bursting cauldron, pouring from every chink, every crevice, a cloud of vapor formed of millions of wings mounting to the blue, in the doubtful and nearly frustrated search for love. Like all else that is dream and illusion, the splendid vision lasts but a moment, the cloud falls heavily to the ground, bestrewing it with wreckage; the festival is over, love has betrayed its promise and death takes its place." [7]

Death indeed. The myriad bodies are devoured by other forms of life, by birds, reptiles, cats and dogs, rodents, ants, dragonflies. Men shovel them up in heaps and eat them roasted or fried. In some countries they are made into pastry. In any event not one of the swarms returns to the termitary from which it set forth. It is a real holocaust, and a peculiarly senseless one at that, for the winged males and females do not mate in the air as does the bee. Instead they fall to the ground and gnaw off one another's wings. Then, like a lady and gentleman in a proper Victorian novel, they go for a walk. They do not copulate during the walk or even after it, for their first preoccupation is to find a new house. Having gnawed their way into a piece of rotten wood they continue to live together, as Escherich puts it, as virginal maidens and youths. "This 'engagement period,'" he adds, "probably has few analogies in the animal kingdom."

The male and female termites can afford to take their time. They may live as long as twelve years and during this period the female, at the height of her fecundity, may lay an egg every two seconds. The early stage of termite marriage is characterized by complete equality of the sexes. Both build the first cells for the new nest, both care for the eggs and feed the larvae. The future workers and soldiers develop slowly. In some species almost a year must elapse before they are able to aid their parents. In this respect the termite differs from the bee, in which only twenty-one days is needed to form a worker.

Once the colony has reached a certain size the male and female (inaccurately referred to as king and queen, for they do no ruling) withdraw to a central chamber and devote themselves exclusively to breeding. The female is transformed into a veritable monster, indeed the whole scene in the "royal chamber" has a monstrous quality as the following account suggests.

"Beneath a low, murky dome, vast in comparison with the size of the normal insect, there sprawls, filling it almost entirely, like a whale surrounded by minnows, the enormous, flabby, inert, greasy, whitish mass of the appalling idol. Thousands of worshippers are incessantly licking and fondling the monster; but not, it would seem, quite disinterestedly, for the royal exudation appears to be so seductive that the little soldiers forming the bodyguard are hard put to it to prevent zealots from carrying off a morsel of the divine skin to satisfy their passion, or it may be their appetite. Old queens are covered with glorious scars, and look as though they had been patched and repatched.

"Around the insatiable mouth hundreds of tiny workers are busily feeding her with the pap it is her privilege to receive; while at the other end another crowd has collected to gather from the oviduct, and wash and carry away, the eggs as they drop out. And in the midst of this turbulent multitude little soldiers are circulating to keep order, whilst ringed round the sanctuary, with their backs to it, formed up in perfect line to face a possible enemy, warriors of lofty stature, their mandibles ready, constitute a motionless, menacing guard." [6]

The male lives with the female but is transformed into a shabby, puny, furtive, little creature forever scuttling under the great white dumpling of the queen's belly where he presumably contrives to mate with the giantess. This goes on year after year and, in some species, results in the production of 11 million eggs a year, each of which has its destiny decided by some mysterious force that maintains the balance between soldiers, workers and the winged males and females destined later to swarm. This balance is evidently maintained by special hormones (pheromones).

Finally the queen ages and her egg production declines, her devoted attendants lose interest in her, stop supplying her with food. She dies of starvation. At once the huge helpless body is set upon and the remains are devoured with relish, as are all other corpses in the termitary. The lost queen is replaced by a younger egg-layer of whom several are kept in reserve within the termitary and the endless round of egg-laying continues.

HERMAPHRODITE LOVE

Although the production of sperm by one individual and of eggs by another is the pattern of sex among the vertebrates, several creatures without backbones deviate from this pattern. Here we find a condition which recalls the myth of Hermaphroditus, the lovely son of Hermes and Aphrodite who was indissolubly united with a water nymph at the Carian fountain and who thus combined in one body both male and female. Hermaphrodite animals occasionally fertilize themselves, following the example of the violet, that arch-hypocrite among the plants. More often they couple with another member of the same species. The problem they are confronted with is which shall play the role of male and which the role of female, which shall donate the sperm and which receive it. Among earthworms there is no argument. They lie together head to tail, perfectly aligned, the male opening in the fifteenth segment close to the saddle or clitellum of the other worm. Each worm donates sperm to the other worm but these sperm do not at once seek out the eggs. They are stored in special sacs called *seminal receptacles.* Only after the worms have separated does the clitellum covering segments thirty-two to thirty-seven secrete a horny ring containing eggs which passes along the earthworm and picks up the sperm from the seminal receptacles. Fertilization occurs as the ring moves on. Finally it slips over the head end of the worm, closes up and forms a cocoon.

Slugs and snails are also commonly hermaphrodite. The force that draws them together is just as obscure as that which attracts the coupling earthworms. If one is both male and female, like the original androgynes of Plato's myth, what need does one have to seek satisfaction from another? Yet it is clear from their behavior that these hermaphrodites do seek others. The sea snail (commonly known as the sea hare) engages in a veritable orgy of sexual togetherness when the breeding season arrives. One sea hare mounts another, playing the male, and donates its spermatophore. Meanwhile a third sea hare mounts the second. Sea hare number three is mounted by a fourth, the fourth by a fifth, the fifth by a sixth, the sixth by a seventh. Finally sea hare one, the only member of the group deprived of the chance to play the role of male, completes the circle by mounting sea hare number seven. Thus do these lowly mollusks far outdo the feats of the *Spintriae*, whose capacity to interlace sexually in groups of three so intrigued the Emperor Tiberius on the island of Capri.

The Roman snail, *Helix pomatia* (the *escargot* of the French gourmet), has been placed at or near the top in the scale of sex energy. Its sexual behavior, from a mammalian point of view, is strange, perverse, topsy-turvy, lopsided and intense. To begin with it has its sex organs in its head, far removed from the orifice through which the body's wastes are voided and which, in all vertebrates, is more or less intimately associated with the genital organs. So the snail's love life is cephalic and untainted. It is also passionate and rich, with a richness that no mere mammal can ever experience. For the snail is a hermaphrodite, has both male and female organs and uses both at the same time, experiencing both the active thrill of the male and the passive sensations of the female (Fig. 12). "Its penis," writes Herbert Wendt in *The Sex Life of the Animals,* "is a gigantic erectile generative tube and its wooing is more passionate and tempestuous than any human Casanova's. Moreover, the creature is apparently inclined to sadism. For after a wild love dance in which the partners rear up sole to sole, rock back and forth and even exchange regular smacking kisses, the excited snail suddenly releases a dagger of chalky material from a kind of quiver and drives it into the body of its mate. Other varieties shoot arrows of chalk at their victim-mates, and these are not aimed at the genital orifice, but are merely intended to wound some part of the mate's body. The wounded snail visibly twitches with pain, and indeed the act seems like the prelude to a veritable sex murder. In fact the love daggers of the Roman and garden snails occasionally penetrate the lung or the abdominal wall of their partners, inflicting deadly wounds.

"But so far we have described only one of the mates. The

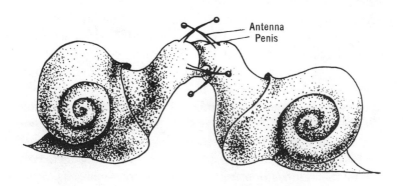

12. *Mating of snails. The snail has both male and female sex organs and uses both at the same time.*

other behaves in exactly the same way during the sex act. It, too, is extremely excited, and its excitement mounts when it is struck by the love arrow. Whereupon the masochist likewise becomes a sadist; it too fires a dart or stabs with a dagger at the body of its partner. It too protrudes a huge penis. And after fierce efforts and writhings, each of the two inserts its member into the genital orifice of the other.

"For several minutes the snails remain united in this mutual copulation. The male organ must penetrate as deeply as possible into the female genital canal in order to deposit the semen at the right place, in a bladder-shaped receptacle where it will fertilize the eggs some time later. Each partner in this act is both male and female. And both seem to discharge sperm at the same time. Then they separate and both snails drop exhausted to the ground, where they remain lying almost motionless for some time. At last they crawl away, each in a different direction." [7]

LOVE AT ARM'S LENGTH

Strange are the ways of the mollusks! Their habit of possessing both sexes and of enjoying the thrills of male and female love simultaneously may be regarded as an improvement on plain heterosexual love. But this practice is not employed by the most highly evolved members of the group. These advanced species are the cephalopods, including the octopus, squid and the chambered nautilus of poetic fame ("Build thee more stately mansions, O my soul"). They are very intelligent beasts and sometimes very large, attaining, in the case of the giant squid, a length of up to sixty feet. Popular mythology has depicted them as hideous monsters, sending out their enormous tentacles like serpents from the sea, clutching small boats and dragging them down to their doom. Actually they are far less aggressive than the humans they

are reputed to attack. Tales are told to illustrate their cleverness, their emotionality, their love of dancing. The octopus
seizes stones in its tentacles to break open mussels. The squid
invented jet propulsion and the smoke screen. (It uses sepia
but the principle is the same.) A squid imprisoned alone in
an aquarium suffers from melancholia, kills itself by devouring
its own arms. Embracing squids rock and roll in such a fashion
that the observer is reminded of certain popular dances.

Cephalopods were much admired by the Greeks who found
in these agile, highly symmetrical invertebrates an endless
source of inspiration for artistic representations and myths.
They were models for the Hydra and the Gorgon, they appear
with tentacles gracefully intertwined on innumerable vases.
The love lives of these beasts were studied by Aristotle who
was familiar with the common squid and the cuttlefish, both
of them plentiful in the Mediterranean. He describes them
"with mouths and tentacles facing one another and fitting
closely together." He realized that the sexes were separate
(these creatures are not hermaphrodite), but was hazy as to
where the male kept its sex organ and how it was used. "Some
assert that the male has a kind of penis in one of his tentacles;
and they further assert that the organ is tendinous in character,
growing attached right up to the middle of the tentacle, and
that the latter enables it to enter the nostril or funnel of the
female."

Aristotle was not far wrong. The males of all types of cephalopods have evolved special tentacles (hectocotylus) which
serve as instruments of procreation. The way in which they
use these instruments varies greatly. In some forms such as
the octopus the male first stimulates the female by letting his
copulatory arm play over her body. That this activity arouses
sexual excitation may be seen from the lively color changes
that both partners display, with the erotic color red predomi-
nating. After prolonged stroking, when the male feels that the
correct moment has come, he reaches with the copulatory arm

into his mantle cavity, withdraws several packages of semen and thrusts these into the mantle cavity of the female (Fig. 13). These attentions may not prove entirely welcome to the female, for the opening into which the copulatory arm has been thrust is actually her breathing funnel. Furious battles may therefore develop between the copulating pair if the female feels she is being asphyxiated by her lover. Once inside the female's body the packets of sperm burst and the spermatozoa are poured over the eggs. In some forms the hectocotylus breaks off inside the mantle cavity, remains there until the eggs are ready for fertilization, then discharges its sperm. The rest of the copulatory arm is absorbed into the female's body.

Strangest of all is the copulatory pattern of the paper nautilus, *Argonauta argo*. The mantle cavity of this form, whose paperlike shell was thought by the Greeks to be the cradle of the foam-born Aphrodite, was often found to be crawling with worm-shaped, highly active creatures. Aristotle thought they

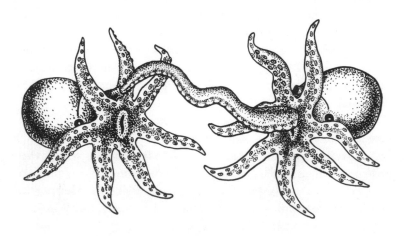

13. Mating of squids. The male withdraws several packages of semen and thrusts these into the mantle cavity of the female.

were parasitic worms and they were later given a special name, *Hectocotylus*, by Cuvier. It was not until 1853 that Johannes Muller finally discovered that these long whiplike objects were actually the copulatory arms of the nautilus male. The male in this form is a dwarf, only about one-tenth the size of the female and its copulatory arm is rolled up in a pear-shaped bladder. This bladder bursts and liberates the arm which appears to break off and swim freely in the sea. These "swimming penises" have, Herbert Wendt observes, "caused zoologists a great deal of perplexity. Does the nautilus male send his arm out to seek a bride? Does he detach it and let it swim to the female on its own? That would certainly be a remarkable form of procreation-at-a-distance." [7]

It would indeed! Of all the strange manifestations of sex energy this is one of the strangest, for what can guide the detached copulatory arm, eyeless and brainless, to its journey's end? However, it must be admitted that no one has actually seen such an arm swim to a female nautilus and crawl into her mantle cavity. Perhaps the free-swimming arms found in the ocean have accidentally slipped out of the female's body after mating.

The practice of mating at arm's length is not confined to squids. Newts manifest in their sexual relations a remoteness such as might lead one to suppose that they shared the opinions of the Fathers of the Church on the subject of carnal lust. The male newt does not touch the female. Instead, decked out in his colorful mating costume, he poses and struts before her on a level area in the bottom of some pond. At a certain critical moment he produces his packet of sperm. The female is properly aroused by his mating dance, picks up the sperm pack with her cloaca. There is no kiss, no caress, only a dance. But the dance is important. If the sperm pack is presented to the female in the absence of the cavorting male she merely ignores it.

LOVE IN THE WATER

The impartial biologist may regret that the hermaphrodite pattern of sexual behavior did not persist beyond the level of such invertebrates as the snail. To be able to play the role of either male or female, to be capable both of giving and receiving, of possessing and being possessed, of ejecting semen and elaborating eggs would certainly add zest and variety to that "ludicrous pattern of engagement," as one authority (Lawrence Durrell) has dubbed the human copulatory act. Also, on purely aesthetic grounds, one may regret that the pattern we see in the snail, the spider or the squid, in which the sexual function is separated from that of excretion, failed to become established among vertebrates. Had it done so we can feel reasonably sure that those absurd concepts, indecency and obscenity, would not have arisen to bedevil certain woolly-minded members of the human race. The words "dirty" and "filthy," so commonly used in connection with sexual behavior, clearly show that the distaste man feels for his excrements has rubbed off on the sexual function and contaminated an act which is in itself quite clean and inoffensive. This problem would not have arisen if men, like squids, had sex organs on the end of their arms and could offer their sperm to the female with no more danger of fecal contamination than is involved in shaking hands. Thus sex and shit would have been kept separate and learned judges would not have to waste vast amounts of time trying to decide whether the scribblings of some poet or peasant could properly be defined as filthy, pornographic and obscene.

This did not happen. With the development of the vertebrate pattern a link was established between defecation, urination and reproduction decreed by a force the aim of which (it seems) was to keep the number of body openings to a minimum. Sperm and urine were voided through a common duct (the urethra), often by a special organ (the penis). Entrance to the female tract became localized *inter feces et urinam* and birth took place through the same lowly chamber, a fact that impressed St. Augustine as offering irrefutable evidence of the fallen state of man.

It would not be correct to suppose that the copulatory thrill generated by the insertion of the penis into the vagina is the universal bribe dangled before all vertebrates by nature to compel them to breed. Many male vertebrates do not even possess a penis and some are as careless in their reproductive habits as the American oyster. The female cod makes no attempt to find a mate, pours forth millions of eggs into the ocean, only a few of which are fertilized and even fewer reach maturity. Other fish are drawn together at mating time by some force not dependent on any copulatory bribe. The little three-spined stickleback provides an example. The male stickleback makes a nest, a tunnel in a mass of water weeds. Having finished his nest he turns a bright red, begins at once to court any female that swims into view. Such females are swollen with fifty to one hundred large eggs and swim toward the male in a curious head-up posture. He leads her into the nest and prods her tail base which causes her to lay her eggs. She swims out of the nest, the male swims in, deposits his sperm, then chases the female away and looks for another partner. As many as five females may deposit their eggs in the nest. The male fertilizes them all. His mating impulse then subsides, his red color vanishes, he becomes hostile to females, devotes himself instead to protecting the young which he carries around in his mouth.

Among fish, as among many other vertebrates, courtship display provides the key that enables the male to distinguish between a female and another male. The same energy, it appears, that leads to mating when male meets female explodes into furious hostility if male meets male. This is clearly seen among Siamese fighting fish. When the male fish, ready for mating, encounters another fish of the same species he begins what Konrad Lorenz calls a self-display dance. He swims around his presumptive mate in a state of excitement, revealing his glowing colors and the iridescent rays in his beautiful fins. It remains for a time uncertain whether this display will lead to love overtures and mating or to a bloody battle which Lorenz describes as follows:

"On account of their beauty, the fighters appear less malevolent than they really are and one is just as loath to ascribe to them embittered courage and contempt of death as one is to associate head-hunting with the almost effeminately beautiful Indonesian warriors. Nevertheless, both are capable of fighting to the death . . . When they are stimulated to the point of inflicting the first sword-thrust, it is only a matter of minutes till wide slits are gaping in their fins, which in a few more minutes are reduced to tatters. The method of attack of a fighting fish, as of nearly all fish that fight, is literally the sword-thrust and not the bite. The fish opens its jaws so wide that all its teeth are directed forward, and in this attitude, it rams them, with all the force of its muscular body, into the side of its adversary. The ramming of a fighting fish is so strong and hard that its impact is clearly audible if, in the confusion of the fight, one of the antagonists happens to hit the glass side of the tank. The self-display dance can last for hours but if it develops into action, it is often only a matter of minutes before one of the combatants lies mortally wounded on the bottom." [8]

If the displaying male fish encounters a female she may make off in the opposite direction or, if the resplendent male pleases her, approach him "with shy insinuating movements, that is to say in an attitude directly opposed to that of the swaggering male. And now begins a love ceremonial which, if it cannot compare in grandeur with the male war dance, can emulate it in grace of movement" (Lorenz). The male lures the female to a nest of foam which he has prepared by diligently blowing bubbles until the surface of the water is as frothy as a mug full of beer. Swimming in graceful curves the two approach closer to one another until finally the male embraces the female, turns her on her back and ejects his sperm. The female lays her eggs and the male catches them in his mouth. He deposits them in the foam which functions as a nest.

Fish, as Lorenz observes, though technically cold-blooded, are anything but cold in their sexual behavior. Referring to "the wild ecstasies of the fight and of love," he declares that, with the exception of the wild canary, "I know of no animal that can excel in hot-bloodedness a male stickleback, a Siamese fighting fish, or a chiclid." Moreover, these vertebrates, so remote from us on the evolutionary tree, parody human behavior when it comes to making love. No other couples, not even human lovers, kiss with more enthusiasm than the so-called kissing guranis who seize one another's lips with such vigor that often shreds of skin can be seen hanging from these parts and whose kisses may endure for as long as twenty-five minutes. As for courtship displays, these are not necessarily confined to the male. Among pipefish, relatives of the sea horses, it is the female who wears the brightest nuptial dress. It is she who stimulates the male, coaxing him into various erotic games, stirring his passions by displays so artful that Wendt has compared them to the seductive arts and slow disrobing of an experienced courtesan. Finally the female completely entwines the male's body and so excites him that his discharge of semen takes place at the same time as her release of her eggs. Nor do fish disdain patterns of behavior that are regarded as perverse in some human circles. Thus there are supposed to be sheatfish that actually suck the sperm from the male and spit it out on the emerging eggs.

When it comes to intimate embracing few vertebrates can equal the feats of the angler fish. These fish have a line and a lure like a fisherman's rod and line, the lure being dangled in front of their hideous mouths. This equipment is used by the female to attract small fish which are swiftly snapped up and eaten. The male is small enough to make a meal for the female but he avoids her lure and instead attaches himself to her body. Here he remains, in some species undergoing changes that turn him into a mere degenerate wart on the female's skin. He loses teeth, jaws, gills and fins, draws his food directly from the female's blood (Fig. 14). This is the ultimate form of union with the beloved. A more intimate fusion can hardly be imagined. There is, however, no actual copulation. The female lays her eggs; the male expels his sperm. Fertilization is external.

THE LONG SQUEEZE

If sex energy works powerfully among certain fish its manifestations are stranger and stronger among frogs. Again we must realize that the copulatory thrill generated by interaction of penis and vagina plays no role in enticing a male and female frog to unite. The male frog has no penis, the female frog has no vagina. Nature in these forms has practiced the ultimate economy in body openings, making one and the same vent

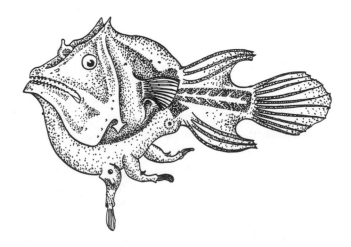

14. Mating of angler fish. The male turns into a degenerate wart on the female's skin.

serve for the waste products from the bowel and the kidneys, as well as the products of the ovaries and the testicles. This common vent is named a cloaca, from the Latin word for sewer, and it serves both birds and amphibia as outlet for body wastes and sex cells.

After the long fast of winter the male frog emerges from hibernation in a state of hormone-induced hunger. He hungers not for food but for something to clasp. He will clasp almost anything provided it is of the right size and shape, a piece of wood, a human hand, another male frog. He does not have the power to distinguish male from female but the male frog when clasped utters a warning croak and the clasper promptly seeks another partner. This seeking is performed amid an almost deafening clamor, for frogs are among the world's noisiest lovers. "Each species of frog has its own call. They croak, squawk, grunt, bleat, thrum, chirp, and whistle; they ring like small bells, knock like hammers, clang like struck iron. And they produce all these sounds by means of the simple method which enables human beings to speak: they make their breath pass over vocal cords.

"When the males at breeding time have noisily proclaimed their desires long enough, the spawn-filled females come hopping or swimming along. Thereupon the males are seized by a rapist's fury. Theirs is no tender courtship; they do not indulge in the games or dances of fish and salamanders. Their sole impulse is to mount upon the female's back and fasten their arms around her in a seemingly irresistible embrace." [7]

This embrace, called the amplexus, may last for days (Fig. 15). The couple behave as if they had been glued together. They hop and waddle over fields and paths in such numbers that the ground under foot is slippery with their bodies. Their tight embrace exposes them to danger for, encumbered as they are, they can move only with difficulty. They are squashed under foot, devoured by storks and herons, but still they cling. At last the female finds a suitable body of water in which to lay her eggs, a process which is aided by pressure of the male's thumbs which sometimes squeeze the female so forcefully as to bore holes in her abdomen. The prolonged sexual orgy is followed by deep exhaustion, for the frogs' reserves have been seriously depleted and a whole summer of hearty eating is needed to rebuild them.

In some species (the midwife toad) the male actually drags the eggs, which are arrayed in long strings, out of the female's body, fertilizes them, then winds them around his hind legs, keeping them there until the tadpoles hatch. Even queerer is the behavior of the long-nosed frog of Argentina which so intrigued Darwin. Males of this species fertilize the eggs, guard them for two weeks, then suddenly swallow them. They are not cannibals but devoted fathers. The eggs descend not into their stomach but into a special brood pouch which extends from their chins almost to their thighs. They remain in the father's body, nourished by his blood, until they are finished little frogs, at which point they leap forth from the father's mouth and start life on their own.

The male of the marsupial frog also offers obstetrical assistance to the female, fertilizes her eggs and spreads them over her back. Here the tadpoles develop in special pouches. Their emergence, says William Beebe, is one of the most remarkable births among jungle creatures.

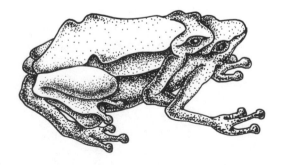

15. Mating of frogs. The embrace may last for several days.

"The opening on the lower back of the frog widened, form-ing the center of a narrow open spindle, as if one should bend apart the thin slats of a venetian blind. A tangle of thickened tissue is pushed out. The frog in the gap was suddenly hustled out by succeeding impatient brethren. He struggled free, did a slide down his mother's bent thigh and somersaulted to the ground. Here he righted himself, looked around and then scraped at his eye where something had lodged. Two scrapes made all well, but no sooner did he gather his feet together and sit upright, exactly as his mother had always sat, than he was knocked head over heels by a brother who rocketed into him. Both rolled over and over, then rerighted, almost touching noses and staring into each other's eyes. . . . Out of the bulg-ing membrane, eyes and snouts began to appear, and some-times four frogs would start a terrific squabble as to which should be born first. The supply seemed unending. There poured out a perfect stream of infants all eager to enter the world and begin their adventures." [9]

SEX, SONG AND TERRITORY

Sex energy, the force which brings male and female together, spills over into acts that are not directly concerned with sexual union. The songs of birds offer an example. These songs have been interpreted as love songs, passionate outpourings by feath-ered Romeos designed to enchant shy Juliets who listen, presum-ably in rapture, to these musical performances. Actually the female songbird could hardly care less about the male's musi-cal performance. The trills and warblings that so enrapture poets have a purely practical aim. They are the statements of a property owner and they declare that trespassers will be prosecuted. They attest to a fact of life, prosaic but funda-mental, which declares that, in a given area, only so many members of a species can settle and breed. This fact, the im-plications of which have been explored by Robert Ardrey in

his book *The Territorial Imperative*,[10] profoundly affects sexual
behavior and the manifestation of the sexual force.

Birds are, of all creatures, the most affected by the territorial
imperative. "The cock," says Wendt, "does not crow to please
the hen, but to inform other cocks: 'Here I am and here I
intend to stay.' Similarly the male finch or lark trills, not to
delight his female, but to set acoustic boundary posts around
his property." Among many species a male without a territory
is a male without a mate. Male wrens, for example, seduce the
females by offering them nests, several of which they build
within their territory. After mating with the female and induc-
ing her to lay her eggs the male loses interest in that particular
mistress, drives her away and entices others to the other nests.
The busy male sings lustily to drive away rivals, cares for and
feeds as many as three different families and rejects monogamy. For him the territory is what matters and the number of
females that wander in and out of it is of secondary interest.
The wren, like Galsworthy's Forsytes, is a "man of property"
but his sense of possession does not extend to his female.

This casual relationship is by no means the rule among
birds. Monogamy, at least for one breeding season, is widely
practiced not for "moral" reasons but for strictly practical ones.
Both parents share the work of incubating the eggs and feeding the offspring. Each recognizes the other and neither will
tolerate a stranger of their own species in the vicinity of the
nest.

The monogamous relationship is taken even further by those
birds that mate for life. Konrad Lorenz, in his fascinating
account of the life of the jackdaw, observed that these birds
pass through a period of "betrothal" before the "marriage."
"The betrothed pair form a heartfelt mutual defense league,
each of the partners supporting the other most loyally. This is
essential, because they have to contend with the competition
of older and higher standing couples in the struggle to take
and hold a nesting cavity. This militant love is fascinating to
behold. Constantly in an attitude of maximum self-display,

and hardly ever separated by more than a yard, the two make their way through life. They seem tremendously proud of each other, as they pace ponderously side by side, with their head feathers ruffled to emphasize their black velvet caps and light gray silken necks. And it is really touching to see how affectionate these two wild creatures are with each other. Every delicacy that the male finds is given to his bride and she accepts it with the plaintive begging gestures and notes otherwise typical of baby birds. In fact, the love-whispers of the couple consist chiefly of infantile sounds, reserved by adult jackdaws for these occasions. Again, how strangely human! With us too, all forms of demonstrative affection have an undeniable childlike tendency—or have you never noticed that all the nicknames we invent, as terms of endearment for each other, are nearly always diminutives?

"The male jackdaw's habit of feeding his wife is a charming gesture which appeals directly to our human understanding, and the chief expression of tenderness shown by the female is no less attractive to our minds. It consists in her cleaning those parts of his head feathers which he cannot reach with his own bill. Friendly jackdaws, as also many other social birds and animals, often perform mutually the duty of 'social grooming,' without any ulterior erotic motive. But I know of no other being which so throws its heart into the process as a lovesick jackdaw lady! For minutes on end—and that is a long time for such a quicksilvery creature—she preens her husband's beautiful, long, silken neck feathers, and he, with sensuous expression and half-shut eyes, stretches his neck toward her. Not even in the proverbial doves or lovebirds does the tenderness of married love find such charming expression as in these notorious corvines. And the most appealing part of their relationship is that their affection increases with the years instead of diminishing. Jackdaws are long-lived birds and become nearly as old as human beings. (Even small birds like warblers or canaries live almost two decades and are still capable of reproduction at the age of fifteen or sixteen years.) Now jackdaws, as described, become betrothed in their first year, marry in their second, so their union lasts long, perhaps longer than that of human beings. But even after many years, the male still feeds his wife with the same solicitous care, and finds for her the same low tones of love, tremulous with inward emotion, that he whispered in his first spring of betrothal and of life." [8]

One of the strangest facts about the sex life of birds results from "imprinting," a process taking place early in a bird's life which irreversibly determines its patterns of behavior. Birds raised by humans regard humans as potential partners in their sexual activities, a fact taken advantage of by the ladies of Rome and mentioned by Catullus in a poem beginning *Passer mortuus est meae puellae.* Lorenz, a bird-lover himself, received love in return from birds he had reared. He was object of the attention of a male house sparrow who "tried by the hour to entice me into my own waistcoat pocket." One of Lorenz's jackdaws (a female) fell in love with a housemaid. A barnyard goose raised among chickens directed all its passion to a Rhode Island cock. Strangest of all the examples offered by Lorenz was that of the male white peacock in the zoo in Vienna who, to save it from perishing of cold, had been raised in the reptile house. For the rest of its life the beautiful bird totally ignored the prettiest peahens and made advances only to giant tortoises!

Mating in birds involves close contact of the cloaca of the male with that of the female. The penis, which plays so important a role in linking male to female, has been developed only by a few species of birds (ostrich, emu, ducks). Most male birds possess only a small papilla at the end of the male duct and successful sperm transfer from male to female depends on accurate alignment of anus with anus. This is rendered more difficult by the profuse growth of tail feathers that is interposed between mounting male and mounted female. Indeed the obstacles are formidable and it seems a wonder that the life-giving transfer takes place at all.

That it does take place is due to a series of actions that follow one another as surely as do the motions of a mechanical doll. The female turkey, for example, is stimulated first by the display put on by the male. In addition to gobbling and developing a fine shade of crimson in the head region the male spreads his tail, trails his wings, and makes short rushing movements. This spectacle triggers the mating reactions of the female which occur in the following series. First, she crouches with head next to her body. Second, she raises her head in response to the weight of the male who has mounted her back. Third, she elevates her tail, responding to pressure of the male's body on the base of the tail. This completes the female's response. If the male has not ejaculated by this time she will wriggle away from beneath him.

As for the male he is guided in his behavior by step two in the female's response. If she fails to raise her head he becomes quite disoriented. When offered a choice between a severed head and a body, male turkeys invariably attempted to copulate with the head! [11]

The peculiarities of avian anatomy make it important that the female actively cooperate if insemination is to occur. For this reason courtship plays a prominent part in the love life of birds. The males cavort and display. They show off their plumage. They offer bribes. They even, in the case of the bower birds, create works of art, erecting structures which look like little huts, paving them with pretty pebbles, even daubing the walls with red clay and decorating them with snail shells, beetle wings, parrot feathers, flowers, leaves, colored seeds. Near human habitations these bower builders steal tinsel, bits of glass, colored paper. The males spend weeks or months building the bowers and finally by loud calls and spirited dance steps invite the females to inspect the work. The display is a part of the courtship ritual and the female is prone to choose as a mate the builder of the most artistic bower.

Among birds that have developed the penis such refined courtship behavior is less in evidence. Ducks provide an example. They pair in the autumn and may start copulating as early as September even though they are mere adolescents and their sex glands are quite undeveloped. By spring the male duck develops his full display plumage and turns, as Wendt puts it, "into a thoroughgoing lecher."

"Male mallards have only one interest in life at this time: they want to copulate with every female they catch sight of. Yet they have not the slightest inclination to loosen the bonds of their marriage and find a new spouse. The couple remains together, feeding in some pond, but keeping an eye out for other mallards—the female because she fears the violence of strange drakes, the male because he wants to overpower and rape the mates of other drakes. Once he has spied the wife of a neighbor, no matter how invitingly his own mate behaves he pays her no heed; he rises into the air and lands in the water beside the strange female.

"From March to May over the ponds of city parks mallards may be seen flying behind one another in groups of three—the female in the van, closely followed by two males. The female utters long-drawn-out cries of alarm. The males persist in their pursuit. It may look as if two rival drakes are chasing an unmated female. But in reality a faithful wife is being pursued by a strange male. The third duck is the rightful husband who joins the chase so that he can find his wife later. Except for staying with her, the husband does not protect his wife from molestation. She, however, does everything in her power to escape from the pursuer. She flies faster, hides in the bushes, or strikes out at the stranger until she is utterly exhausted. Some mallard females will sooner let themselves be drowned than yield to the stranger's lust." [7]

THE PATH TO THE PENIS

Of all the varieties of sexual union the most familiar to humans involves the insertion of a male penis into a female vagina. All mammals use this technique. Some birds employ it. Among insects it has reached incredible levels of refinement. It is also employed by such hermaphrodite mollusks as the Roman snail. Clearly a device so widely employed, developed by so many and various forms of life, must offer great advantages to its possessor. The pattern of life on this planet has favored the development of penises. We will now consider why.

The penis is, above all, an economy measure. By enabling the male to introduce his sperm directly into the female's body it makes possible a great reduction in the number of eggs she must produce. Egg production is a strain, for the egg is always larger than the sperm, loaded with food material, the yolk, which provides for the early growth of the embryo. In mammals such as man the amount of this food material in the egg is small. The mammalian egg exists independently only for a day or so as it rolls down the uterine tube. As soon as it arrives it burrows into the juicy walls of the uterus, develops a placenta and sucks its food from the mother's bloodstream. The situation is very different among birds. Layer upon layer of yolk is added as the egg passes along the oviduct until the final structure may contain over a gallon of fluid (ostrich egg). The production of such massive objects puts a considerable strain on the mother's body. Obviously steps must be taken to ensure that the eggs produced with such effort do not perish unfertilized. The sperm must be introduced into the female body, the male must be equipped with a penis with which to introduce them. The urges necessary to compel him to use the organ must be made an integral part of his behavior.

The penis is a symbol of masculinity, generally thought of as an exclusive possession of the male. Nature, however, has at least once experimented with the reverse arrangement, as if to show that, where sex is concerned, there is no limit to her capacity for variety. This reversal occurs among those quaint aquatic animals whose resemblance to an animate knight in chess has earned them the name sea horses. It is in the sea horse, dweller in the seaweed jungles of tropical oceans, that nature has tested the method of letting the female introduce her eggs into the body of the male (Fig. 16).

"Two sea horses ready for mating put on the tenderest and most charming of courtship spectacles. As among the closely related pipefish, the female is the active partner. In her resplendent wedding dress, far showier than the modest male, she dances around her mate and grasps him with her prehensile tail. Both swim through the water, head against head, in a close embrace, like human lovers. They sway to every side, rock back and forth, and then rise to the surface of the sea. Thereupon something altogether extraordinary happens. The male puffs up his abdomen so that it presents a kind of sac, and the female protrudes a sort of penis from her body.

"This female 'penis' is actually a prolonged genital papilla,

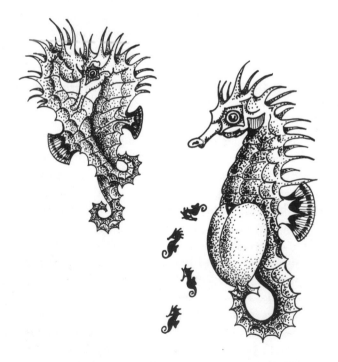

16. *Mating of sea horses. Here nature tests the method of letting the female introduce her eggs into the body of the male.*

usually of a striking orange-red hue. With it, the female gropes about along the male's body and tries to introduce it into an opening in his abdominal sac. An observer of this process cannot help feeling that the male is being fertilized by the female. But what is taking place is not breeding in the proper sense of the word, but only a transmission of eggs. The female wants to deposit her spawn in the male's pouch. Again and again she thrusts her organ into the opening in the pouch and drops one egg after another inside. This act apparently exerts an irresistible stimulus upon the male. For at the same moment that the female's 'penis' enters his body, he pours his sperm into the brood pouch.

"After a while the couple terminate their embrace. The female swims away, but the male sea horse has been 'impregnated' and must now undertake the nourishing and raising of the brood. He continues to behave like a female. The embryos develop in his brood pouch. They hatch out there. And as the small sea horses grow, the father's abdominal region swells like a balloon. At last the 'difficult hour' approaches—the hour of birth.

"The expulsion of the young from the pouch is an ordeal for the sorely tried father—a true delivery. For the opening of the pouch is small and the offspring numerous. The male doubles up, plainly suffers pain, and breathes easier when the last of his children sees the light." [7]

The sea horse is exceptional. In all other forms where sex cells are transferred it is the male that has developed the intromittent organ and this organ, the penis, generally endowed with special erectile power, is the focus of the manifestation of sex energy. The most fundamental manifestation of this energy is the urge which compels the male to insert his penis into the body of the female and the female to receive that organ. The whole stupendous scrimmage called sexual love, with its overtones, undertones, modifications and perversions, rotates about this central act like a colorful carousel about its central steam engine. Any contemporary scientist who has not had his capacity for wonder brainwashed by dreary professors who teach that wonder is not scientific must marvel over the complexity of these interactions. How did a purely random series of mutations ensure that the penis, in every instance, is just the right shape and length, erects itself at just the right angle, penetrates just the right distance to ensure the impregnation of the female of the appropriate species? If anything could tempt the wary scientist to postulate a plan and therefore a planner it would be this matter of penis-fit. The theme is worthy to be celebrated in the works of poets and should be seized upon by theologians as evidence of the existence of a divine artificer.

A FANTASTIC ORGAN

Penises vary enormously in shape and in size, ranging from 2.5 meters in whales to the almost microscopic organs of certain insects. Curiously enough it is not among mammals that this intromittent organ attains its greatest development. If prizes were offered for both length (in relation to body size) and for complexity of penis-design fleas would emerge the champions. "The copulatory apparatus of the male flea is the most elaborate genital organ in the animal kingdom," wrote Miriam Rothschild in a recent article.[12] She went on to say that "an engineer looking objectively at such a fantastically unpractical apparatus would bet heavily against its operational success."

It is indeed fantastic, containing two penis plates, an intromittent organ, the penis proper, a stout penis rod and a thin penis rod. So complicated is the device and so tortuous is the tube in the female's body into which it has to be inserted that the male flea has to use a whole battery of clasping organs heavily armored with spines, struts and hooks to immobilize the female during intromission. The male, in this instance, appears to use brute force to subdue his partner, for female fleas are often seriously injured during copulation. In order to make the connection the male first lines up the intromittent organ opposite the opening of the female's genital organ, the penis proper is then lined up at the correct angle, the thick penis rod is inserted and guided (Venus alone knows how) around a U turn into a minute hole at the side of the oviduct and into a sac called the *bursa copulatrix* (Fig. 17). The thin penis rod picks up the sperm, twisting them around like spaghetti on the end of a fork. Continuing to elongate, it negotiates a right-angle bend, enters a duct of threadlike fineness, avoids plunging down a dangerous *cul de sac*, negotiates two U turns and finally deposits the sperm in the female's spermatheca where they are extruded when the eggs are laid. Fully extended in this way the flea's penis rod is almost a third as long as its whole body; nevertheless the male flea appears to be able to retract the whole apparatus and lives to copulate again. In this respect it differs from the male bee (drone) who,

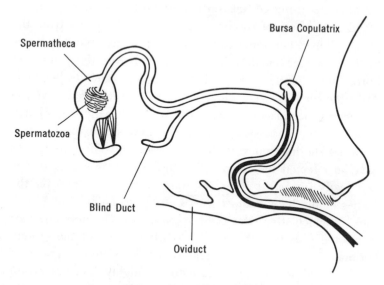

*17. Copulation among fleas. "The copulatory apparatus of
the male flea is the most elaborate genital
organ in the animal kingdom."*

after the thrilling nuptial flight which culminates high in the air in union with the queen, has its entire genital equipment torn out of its body owing to an arrangement of spines which make withdrawal of the penis impossible.

A few further observations may be made about the sex life of the flea. It illustrates elegantly the role played by hormones, those chemical messengers heavily involved in all macrosexual manifestations. The flea's sexual behavior is regulated by the behavior of its host. Rabbit fleas that live on the ears of their hosts feel the excitement of the coming sexual storm as soon as the buck rabbit sets eyes on the doe. When rabbits copulate their temperatures rise, sometimes by as much as 7°C. This amorous fever affects the fleas who become frantically excited and can be seen hopping up and down like cheer leaders, jumping from buck to doe and back again as if urging on the pairing rabbits to greater copulatory ardor. In female rabbits ovulation follows soon after coitus. This is accompanied by an outpouring of sex hormones both from the pituitary gland at the base of the brain (gonadotropins) and from the ovaries. These hormones cause the fleas to cling more ardently to the pregnant female rabbit until just before the young are born. They then leave the rabbit's ears and move to her face. After the birth is over, when the female is licking her young and eating her placenta (as is the habit of many mammalian females), the fleas swarm onto the newborn babies, urged again by the hormones of the female rabbit. These hormones have so affected the female flea that her eggs are now ripe and ready for fertilization. As soon as the fleas land on the bodies of the baby rabbits they indulge in an orgy of bloodsucking which stimulates them to copulate. The hormone that drives the fleas to mate is not a sex hormone but the growth hormone (somatotropin) secreted by the pituitary gland of the baby rabbits. Growth hormone is highly specific; rabbit growth hormone is chemically different from human growth hormone. Because of this, rabbit fleas can breed only on rabbits.

Copulation among insects is often awkward and, from the human standpoint, would seem uncomfortable. The insect penis nearly always points in the wrong direction and the whole organ must be turned inside out before it can be inserted in the female's genital opening. To establish connection the male is compelled to go through a variety of contortions which sometimes prove fatal. The standard procedure is for the male to alight on the female's back, curve his abdomen around and introduce his penis into the vagina. The maneuver is complicated by a flighty tendency insect females have of taking off during copulation, leaving the wretched male dangling by his penis and clasping appendages. In large-winged species the wings get in the way, so moths and butterflies copulate end to end, facing in opposite directions. Some flies curl their abdomens over their shoulders and approach the female from behind. Crane flies mate tail to tail but the male has to twist his body through 180 degrees to assure correct penetration. "Insects," writes Susan Michelmore in *Sexual Reproduction*, "make mating so complicated that it seems a wonder they ever produce any offspring." [13] They are the only group of animals in which it appears to matter which surface of the penis is uppermost when it enters the vagina. Their genital organs are ornamented with such a profusion of bristles, pads, toothlike projections and chitinous plates that they resemble a complex lock and its equally complex key. This serves to ensure that insects can only mate with others of the same species.

SEXUAL ATTRACTANTS

Insects have solved the mate-finding problem in a fashion that humans might envy. A man may go through his whole life without meeting his dream-girl, and a woman may never discover the right mate. There is no method of attraction or advertising available which allows the human to draw to himself the partner he desires. Far better off is the gypsy moth which secretes a chemical substance called gyplure and the female silk moth which advertises her presence with bombykol. These extremely powerful chemical sex advertisements are present in minute amounts in the individual insects. So scant is the substance that Adolf F. J. Butenandt at the Max Planck Institute had to extract a quarter of a million silk moths in order to get enough material to analyze. Martin Jacobson and his co-workers at the U.S. Department of Agriculture had a somewhat easier time with the American cockroach. They simply drew streams of air over cans of cockroaches and condensed the odor by passing the air through chambers immersed in a refrigerant. By this procedure they obtained an analyzable amount of sex attractant from a mere 10,000 female cockroaches.

Writes Edward O. Wilson: "The power of the insect attractants is almost unbelievable." [14] He goes on to state that 0.01 micrograms (one hundred thousand millionths of a gram) of gyplure would be enough, if evenly distributed, to excite a billion male gypsy moths. This almost miraculous power of the chemical sex attractants of insects explains why Jean Henri Fabre, who first studied the phenomenon in the nineteenth century, could not bring himself to believe that the attraction he observed was due to a chemical cause. "One might as well expect," he said "to tint a lake with a drop of carmine." But the male moth's sensitive receptors on its feathery antennae can pick up the scent in the ocean of air even at a considerable distance. At this distance they cannot fly in the direction of increasingly strong scent, for it is equally diluted all around. Instead they instinctively fly against the wind and finally find the source of the chemical lure.

The chemical sex attractants are not confined to insects. Musk (the product of a gland on the musk deer) and civetone (from the civet cat) have long been assumed to have sexual functions. The odor of the male mouse has a synchronizing effect on the estrus cycle of the female mouse, but the odor of other female mice upsets it. The odor of a strange mouse will block the pregnancy of a newly impregnated female mouse but the odor of a male that has mated with that female has no effect. In animals that depend on their sense of smell to establish a relationship with the outer world it is natural that this highly developed sense should play a role in the attraction between the sexes. Man, being sight-dominated, relies more on his eyes than his nose in the quest for a mate.

OTHER PATHS TO THE PENIS

Among vertebrates the path to the penis was approached at an early stage of evolution by the cartilaginous fishes that are collectively known as selachians. These include sharks and rays. They are an old group, primitive but successful (if long survival is a measure of success). The males of these creatures have evolved from their pelvic fins a penislike instrument capable of being introduced into the cloaca of the female. During copulation the male shark wraps itself around the body of the female, completely encircling her like a huge doughnut. After he has widened the female orifice by spreading it with his copulatory fins he extrudes a genital papilla and thrusts it into the female opening, so the females in this group are fertilized internally. In some species the egg develops within the body of the mother and there is even a sort of placenta through which the young are nourished. The young are born alive and are even cared for by their mothers after birth. Thus the lowly shark has approached, where reproduction is concerned, the pattern of the lofty mammals.

The penis proper was developed by the reptiles but tentative approaches were made to this organ by certain snakelike amphibians called caecilia. The process used by these beasts was graphically described by Wilhelm Bolsche, author of

Love Life in Nature, who was the first to publish a popular account of the multiple manifestations of sex energy without either losing his job or being hauled into court on a charge of obscenity.

"Despite their snake form, the aforesaid caecilia has no tail of any kind, but the anus is placed exactly on the posterior tip of the body. Since this anus is at the same time a genuine gateway of love, our blind burrowing friend pushes out the wall of its anus in the form of a long pointed cone, till the anus itself looks like a genuine copulative member. And this it now thrusts deep into the anus of the female burrower, as a really ingenious pederast, in whose case the maneuver still fulfills its real purpose." [15]

The device was further elaborated by male lizards and snakes which evolved forked organs called hemipenes which can be protruded from the anus and inserted into the anus of the female. These organs of copulation, heavily armed with spines, warts and hooks, serve to hook the male so firmly into the female body that mating lizards can be separated only with difficulty. As for the snake, it is so firmly attached that it has to drag its mate along by the anus if the act of union is interrupted and sudden flight becomes necessary (Fig. 18).

The sex act among lizards is characterized by violence and features the "love bite" so commonly found among carnivorous mammals. The ardent male approaches the female and suddenly digs his teeth into her flank or neck. If she tolerates the bite and accepts the male the latter must slide his abdomen underneath her in such a way that the anal slits meet and the spiny hemipenis can be introduced. This element of violence in the sex life of contemporary lizards may set the imaginative biologist to wondering about the matings of those gigantic extinct forms that crashed their way through the swamps of the Jurassic and Cretaceous eras. What were the mating patterns of the brontosaurus with a brain as big as a hen's egg and a body 180 feet long? Did *Tyrannosaurus rex,* the fearsome flesh-eater, also practice the love bite? How in the world did such forms as Ankylosaurus, heavily armored as tanks, ever manage to copulate?

We shall never know the answers to these questions. The genitalia and the copulatory methods of these monsters are alike lost among the debris of the ages. Perhaps they behaved like crocodiles which are rough and crude in their amours. The male crocodile has a copulatory organ which usually lies hidden in the cloacal slit but which, under the influence of sexual excitement, becomes engorged with blood just like a mammalian penis. The males roar and fight when in the grip of the breeding impulse. They display an array of fearsome teeth, they bellow until the swamps resound. Totally lacking in courtesy they heave the females over until they lie on their backs, overpower them and unite with them belly to belly, for the penis of the male crocodile has only a groove, not a tube, down which the semen must flow so that gravitation is involved in the transfer of sperm. Hence the prostration of the female. The male may turn the female the right way up after the act is completed. This is as far as he goes with old-world courtesy.

Male turtles are more chivalrous. They have to be. So heavily

18. *Mating snakes: "So firmly attached that the female
must drag its mate along by the anus if
the act of union is disturbed."*

protected is the female turtle that unless she cooperates fully
the sexual act cannot be performed at all. So turtles dance or
engage in curious quivering movements that excite the female
to the point of extruding the lower part of the body with the
cloacal cleft completely out of the shell. The male climbs on
her back, and bends his own tail sufficiently to enable him to
introduce his copulatory organ into the cloaca of the female.
Land tortoises, the males of which become peculiarly passionate at breeding time, force the female to protrude her tail end
by snapping at the front end. As the female is very fat at
breeding time she cannot withdraw both ends into the shell
at once. She withdraws the front end to avoid her mate's
snappings and has to protrude the rear end whether she likes
it or not. In this position she is promptly mounted by her ardent
lover. In many species of tortoise the males use the spiny tips
of their tails to stimulate the female genital region. They
strike the female cloaca almost continuously while riding on
their mate's back, intensifying by this means the female's sexual excitement so that she extrudes the hind end of her body
as far as possible out of the shell as a result.

MAMMALIAN LOVE

Mammals, following the example of the reptiles, all utilize the
penis as the organ of sexual union. The pattern of mammalian
sex developed gradually. The cloaca, the common sewer, which
for amphibians, birds and reptiles forms the sole exit both for
excrements and for the products of the sex glands, is still found
in such primitive mammals as the duck-billed platypus. In
this creature the male copulatory organ is a simple tube on the
rear wall of the cloaca. Two other unusual mammals, the spiny
anteater and the three-clawed echidna of Australia and New
Guinea, also have this structure. These animals, standing on
the borderline which separates the mammals from the reptiles,
have been called monotremata, "animals with one hole." They

lay eggs and incubate these eggs as do birds. Their only link with the mammals consists in their possessing milk glands.

As the mammals evolved, the cloaca became divided into two openings. The anus, now sole exit of the intestine, retained from the old cloacal days certain sexual associations which make it one of the erogenous zones of the mammalian body. But the focal point of sexual awareness was shifted forward, becoming concentrated on the clitoris of the female and the glans penis of the male.

Nature did not lavish on the mammalian penis the ingenuity she employed in fashioning the penis of the flea. It is nonetheless a remarkable organ. Its power of erection, its curious independence and its capacity to become the focus of intense sensation aroused the wonder alike of Aristotle and Leonardo da Vinci. The penis, wrote the latter in one of his notebooks, "confers with the human intelligence and sometimes has intelligence of itself, and although the will of the man desires to stimulate it, it remains obstinate and takes its own course, and moving sometimes of itself without license or thought by the man, whether he be sleeping or waking, it does what it desires; and often the man is asleep and it is awake, and many times the man is awake and it is asleep; many times the man wishes it to practice and it does not wish it; many times it wishes it and the man forbids it. It seems therefore that this creature has often a life and intelligence separate from the man, and it would appear that the man is in the wrong in being ashamed to give it a name or to exhibit it, seeking rather constantly to cover and conceal what he ought to adorn and display with ceremony as a ministrant."

In all mammals the penis is the prime symbol of masculinity but it is not always the most obvious symbol. Maleness in elephants, spotted hyenas, beavers and gorillas is hard to determine because of the difficulty of finding the penis. The organ comes in various shapes and sizes, varying in length from a few millimeters in small mammals to several feet in the large whales. All mammalian penises possess the property of increasing considerably in size under the influence of sexual excitement, but the amount of this enlargement varies. Penises of the fibroelastic type rely for their rigidity mainly on their cartilaginous components. In carnivores the penis is given additional rigidity by a penis bone. Dogs, ferrets, mink, the walrus and the whale all possess this equipment. Man and the other primates have evolved purely vascular penises whose capacity for erection depends entirely on blood pressure. The organ is peculiarly vulnerable in man who lacks the equipment needed to enable him to withdraw his penis into a protective sheath such as is possessed by the males of most mammalian species.

Though smaller than the great apes man far exceeds them both as regards the length of his penis and the frequency with which he uses it. The huge gorilla has often been represented as a creature burning with lust with a habit of kidnapping women and using them for its sexual pleasure (a myth propounded both by Count Buffon and by Richard Burton, translator of *The Arabian Nights*). Actually the huge ape, according to naturalists who have observed it in the wild, seems hardly interested in sex at all and the male gorilla's sexual equipment is so modest that, even in full erection, it measures a scant two inches.

Omitting man, whose complex amatory exploits will be considered separately, we can follow Dr. H. Hediger in dividing mammals into two groups on the basis of their copulatory behavior.[16] To the first group belong most of the herbivores and such aquatic mammals as whales and dolphins. In this group copulation occurs extremely rapidly. The nilgai, largest of the Indian antelopes, provides an example. When the female is in heat she stops for a moment in front of the male and diverts her tail. The male rises on his hind legs and, without even touching the female's back, inserts his penis for a fraction of a second and all is over. The gerenuk, most elegant of antelopes, copulates so swiftly that the female does not even stop trotting while the pursuing male mounts her. As for the whale, this giant mammal accomplishes its sexual union in midair, during a leap from the water, male and female uniting belly to belly during the instant of leaping, a feat of amatory coordination that few species can equal. The dolphin mates in an equally rapid manner.

To the second group belong various carnivores among which copulation is a time-consuming business. Among both the big cats (lions, tigers, leopards) and the little cats preparations are prolonged and involve much howling and writhing (Fig. 19). Dogs, wolves and coyotes may remain linked for hours after the sexual act has reached its climax because the base of the penis swells to form a large bulb inside the labia and special muscles in the female contract to lock the penis within. Bears may remain coupled for hours or even days, the pair walking about as a six-legged creature.

Aggression and even cruelty are an integral part of mammalian copulation, as is shown by the following passage from *Patterns of Sexual Behavior*: "Male sheep . . . bite the ewe's wool and skin during precoital play. The stallion often nips at the withers of the receptive mare and frequently bites her neck while he is mounted in the position for service. The

19. Mating cats. The male bites the neck of the female.

courtship and mating of some fur-bearing cetaceans involves a good deal of painful stimulation. During copulation, the male elephant seal holds the female by biting her neck. Female sea lions grip the male's neck in their teeth before copulating.

"The normal mating pattern of the mink, marten and sable begins when the male springs upon the female and seizes the skin of her neck in his mouth. His long, sharp canine teeth pass completely through her pelt and his jaws may remain locked for most of the copulatory period. The female's initial response consists of a vigorous attempt to escape, and for a considerable length of time the two animals engage in what appears to be a violent battle. The male is much larger than his mate and when her struggles grow less marked he gets into a position which will permit intromission. Eventually insertion is accomplished, and . . . it may be maintained for several hours. Only after he has penetrated the female is the male likely to relax his grip on her neck, and if she tries to terminate the mating before he is ready to do so, he promptly secures another neck hold and prevents her from escaping.

"This description might appear to justify application of the term 'rape' to copulation in these animals, and the comparison has been proposed many times. In actuality, however, males of these species can never copulate with a female who is truly nonreceptive. The female must respond appropriately to the male, and nonestrous females fail to do so. The violent behavior has an important biological function. Many males refuse to mate with females that are too compliant and therefore fail to offer the normal amount of resistance. If coition takes place without the usual conflict, conception rarely occurs." [17]

MALE ORGAN, HUMAN

The penis in man is a composite organ consisting of two cavernous bodies (the *corpora cavernosa*) and a spongy body (the *corpus spongiosum*) which contains the urethra, a tube connected to the urinary bladder and to the various glands that contribute to the semen (Fig. 20). The *corpus spongiosum* expands to form the *glans penis* at the top of the organ and the bulb of the penis at its base. The whole structure is enclosed in skin which protrudes over the *glans penis* as a protective sheath (the foreskin) but which, owing to its tendency to constrict and to harbor dirt, is apt to do more harm than good. For this reason it has been a practice in certain cultures to remove this foreskin (circumcision), a practice which, for some obscure reason, has become endowed with great religious significance in the Judeo-Christian and Moslem traditions.

The human penis varies in length in the flaccid state from 2.8 to 5.6 inches, but the amount of enlargement which results from erection is not proportional to the flaccid size. The greatest increase in length on erection recorded by Masters and Johnson [18] was in a penis measuring 3 inches in the flaccid state which swelled to 6.6 inches on erection. The smallest

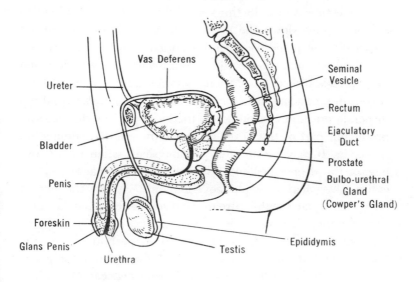

20. Human male sex organs.

increase was in a penis of 4.4 inches which attained the same erect size (6.6) as the smaller organ. It is a curious fact that in man the size of the penis has a less constant relation to the body size than any other organ. After examining 312 men aged between twenty-one and eighty-nine years Masters and Johnson concluded that there is no relation between a man's skeletal framework and the size of his external genitalia. The largest penis in the group measured 5.6 inches in the flaccid state and was owned by a man 5 feet 7 inches tall who weighed 152 pounds. The smallest measured (just over 2.4 inches in the flaccid state) was on a man 5 feet 11 inches tall, weighing 178 pounds.

MALE ORGASM

The penis erects when arteries lining the walls of the cavernous bodies become engorged with blood and swell as a result. At the same time valves in the veins which return the blood to the heart slow down the outflow of blood from the erected organ. So the penis becomes distended for the same reason that a rubber tube connected to a tap becomes distended when the water is turned on. Various nervous impulses may be involved in producing this condition. Sexual excitement resulting in penile erection can originate in the depths of the fantasy-producing part of the brain without any external stimulation whatever. It may be initiated during sleep when the awareness of the sleeper becomes filled with erotic images and the entire physiological sequence commonly called "the act of love" takes place with a dream partner, terminating in emission of semen. It may be excited by the sight of a pretty girl, the touch of a lover, the odor of certain perfumes, even the sound of certain music. Stranger still, this erection of the penis, so vital to the performance of the sexual act, can take place without any sexual stimulation whatever. It regularly occurs during what is called REM (rapid eye movement) sleep without any accompanying sexual fantasy. It occurs in baby boys whose sexual impulses are unformed. It can be provoked by nonsexual emotion, particularly fear, by the need to urinate and by various pathological conditions affecting the brain.

The reaction producing an erection is generally beyond the reach of the will, though some males, like the French writer De Maupassant, claimed to be able to produce an erection on demand. Quite commonly the opposite state of affairs is observed. Erotic literature is filled with the lamentations of would-be lovers whose laggard and totally disobedient penises refused to become erect even under the most promising conditions. So infuriating was this state that our hagridden ancestors habitually attributed it to the effects of witchcraft. Considerable numbers of unfortunate women were burnt alive because some male was unable to generate an erection and became convinced as a result that he was bewitched.

Masters and Johnson distinguish three phases of sexual excitement in the human male corresponding to three degrees of erection of the penis. The first phase involves penile erection of variable intensity. This erection can be maintained for long periods, the degree of tumescence waxing and waning depending on circumstances. Prolonged love play, prior to actual coitus, does not exhaust the erectile power of the normal male penis. The distended organ remains in a state of readiness as long as the stimulation it receives remains at the love play level. It is his capacity to remain in this first phase long enough to ensure the full arousal of his partner that distinguishes the skillful lover from the unskilled. This maintenance of the first stage of erection makes possible the practice of the art of *maithuna* which is also called *coitus reservatus.*

The second stage of erection, called by Masters and Johnson the plateau phase, is ushered in by a still greater increase in the swelling of the male organ. It becomes hotter, and the glans at the end of the penis becomes larger, assuming in many cases a reddish-purple color. During this plateau phase two or three drops of a mucoid secretion appear at the tip of the penis. Most of the mucoid material is thought to be contributed by Cowper's gland, but the mucus has been found to contain actively motile spermatozoa.

At a certain point the plateau phase passes over into stage three, the orgasmic phase. Up to stage three the human male can govern his own reactions to suit those of his partner. He can intentionally reduce the level of his excitement or build it up again as he chooses. But as soon as stage three begins he ceases to have any voluntary control over his reactions. A sense of inevitable orgasm precedes the actual contractions which violently expel the seminal fluid in a series of jets. So strong is the pressure created by the involuntary but coordinated contractions of various muscles that the semen may be spurted as far as two feet from the penis tip. At the same time the breathing accelerates up to forty breaths per minute, the heart rate may reach 180 beats per minute and the blood pressure rises by as much as 100 mm. of mercury (systolic). Powerful contractions of the voluntary muscles are accompanied by involuntary contractions of the rectal sphincter.

After stage three the male enters stage four, the resolution phase, during which sexual excitement ebbs and the penis returns to its flaccid state. The rate at which it does so depends on circumstances. Many men have the capacity to maintain an erection after ejaculation, especially if their partner is unsatisfied and demands further attention. Others become so sensitive in the genital organ that any further activity is impossible until the penis has become completely flaccid, at which point a fresh start can be made. The number of times a man can reach a climax and ejaculate varies greatly with the individual and at different times of a man's life. Masters and Johnson describe an individual who ejaculated three times within ten minutes.

The reproductive organ of the human female consists of a pear-shaped uterus with two uterine horns (Fallopian tubes) which partly enclose with their ends the ovary from which the egg cell is produced (Fig. 21). It is within this uterus that the embryo develops, sucking its nourishment from the blood of the mother through a disk-shaped placenta to which the embryo is connected by its umbilical cord. The uterus is a reproductive organ rather than a sexual organ and it plays no direct role in the sexual act. Its cyclic changes do not provoke estrus or heat as they do among the females of so many other mammals, though they may affect the intensity of a woman's desire. During the first part of each menstrual cycle the uterus builds up a thick layer of tissue called the endometrium, a bed for the fertilized egg, the bloodsucking parasite whose advent it awaits. If the bloodsucker fails to materialize, the uterus sheds the entire layer, casting it out via the vagina, a messy, bloody and totally unnecessary embarrassment for the human female that should prove to the open-minded that the force we call "nature" is totally lacking in consideration. (In the majority of primate females the endometrium is absorbed back into the bloodstream and there is no external menstrual flow. There seems no sound physiological reason why such reabsorption should not take place in the human female, saving her from much pain and mess, as well as the stigma of "uncleanness" and its many consequences.)

The mouth of the uterus, the cervix, opens into a muscular sheath, the vagina, which provides a connecting link between the womb and the outside world. The uterus is sterile but the vagina swarms with bacteria and sometimes harbors fungi and protozoa which cause inflammation and produce much discomfort (vaginitis). The interior of the vagina is normally quite acid and this acidity helps to prevent the growth of harmful organisms. The vagina performs three functions: it receves the male organ, it provides a receptacle for the semen and it offers a pathway to the outer world for the contents of the uterus. These uterine contents may take the form of a full-term fetus weighing twelve pounds or more, so the vaginal tube has to be enormously elastic. It is, in the words of Masters and Johnson, "infinitely distensible from a clinical point of view." In a woman who has not had a baby the vagina measures 2.8 to 3.2 inches in length and 0.8 inches in diameter. This "resting measurement" changes under the influence of sexual excitement.

Guarding the opening of the vagina are the major labia which normally conceal and protect all those delicate structures that constitute the external genitals of the human female. These structures include the minor labia, the outlet of the vagina, the glans of the clitoris and the opening of the urethra, a tube leading to the urinary bladder. Of these the minor labia

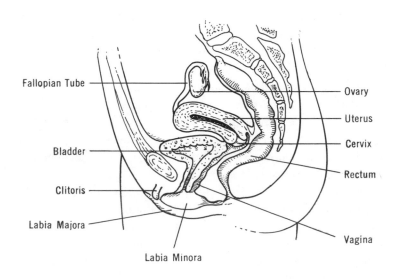

21. Human female sex organs.

and the clitoris are most directly concerned with sexual responses.

The clitoris has been defined as "a unique organ in the total of human anatomy" that appears to have no other function than to initiate and elevate levels of sexual tension. It has been called, and actually is, the homologue of the penis, but whereas the penis is biologically necessary for reproduction (the instrument whereby the seed is sown), the clitoris has no such function. Like the penis it consists of two cavernous bodies enclosed in a capsule, it is attached to the bones of the pelvis by the ischiocavernous muscle and it terminates in the clitoral glans. The organ has an average length of 0.6 inches but varies greatly in size. It is overhung and protected by the clitoral hood which is an extension of the minor labia.

FEMALE ORGASM

During sexual excitement the various organs of the female undergo changes just as pronounced as those undergone by the male, but not so observable. Indeed it is only due to the studies of Masters and Johnson, who were bold enough to set themselves the task of studying the phenomena about which "science develops its sole timidity," that we can describe some of these changes with any precision. For where Kinsey and Company talked, Masters and Johnson measured and photographed and, as a result, we can tell fairly accurately what takes place within the body of the female partner during "that routine rhythm that shakes the world" (Nabokov's phrase).

In the female, as in the male, four stages of sexual response can be distinguished: the excitement phase, the plateau phase, the orgasmic phase, the resolution phase. Sexual excitement shows itself first in the production of vaginal lubrication. "The male gets stiff, the female gets wet." The walls of the vagina seem to sweat and present a picture akin to that of a perspiration-beaded forehead. The reaction is often rapid. In a matter

of seconds a woman may develop sufficient lubrication to fa-
cilitate the insertion of the penis. Other women, the "slow reac-
tors," take much longer to generate the needed lubricant, may
do so only after prolonged foreplay. In such cases the overeager
male may encounter much difficulty in gaining an entrance.
The frigid woman fails to produce this lubricant at all.

As the excitement phase continues the vaginal barrel expands in its upper reaches, ballooning out to such an extent
that the astonished male may feel himself to be "hanging in
midair," an unsatisfactory sensation because it drastically re-
duces the amount of sexual stimulation received by the sensitive tip of the penis. This capacity of the vagina to dilate is
not ordinarily under voluntary control but certain gifted females have acquired the art of filling the organ with air and
generating various sounds.

The excitement phase involves other organs as well as the
vagina. The minor labia become engorged with blood and
the major labia also become strongly distended, flattened and
pushed away from the vaginal opening. The glans of the
clitoris increases in size but this tumescence cannot be correctly termed "erection of the clitoris" because nothing similar
to erection of the penis is normally involved. The engorgement
of the clitoris proceeds parallel to the swelling of the minor
labia and both organs may become twice their normal size.
In addition to these changes in the sex organs there occurs
during the excitement phase an erection of the nipples and
enlargement of the breasts. The "sex flush" may appear in
some women, starting in the region of the stomach and spreading rapidly over the breasts.

As the excitement phase passes into the plateau phase the
lower part of the vagina becomes swollen with blood which
tightens the hold of this organ on the penis. The upper reaches
of the vagina expand still further. The engorged minor labia
undergo vivid color changes during the plateau phase, becoming first pink, then bright red and finally, in some women,
a rich purple. So specific are these color changes that Masters

and Johnson have called the minor labia the "sex skin" of the responding woman. They carefully point out that this sex skin should not be confused with the vivid color changes that occur in baboons and other apes when the female is in heat. No human female can rival the vividness of these displays. The coloration of the sex skin is directly proportional to the effectiveness of the kind of sexual stimulation a woman is receiving. The more intense the stimulation the more brilliant the color change. Furthermore this color change is the surest sign of the approach of orgasm. No woman in Masters' and Johnson's study ever attained orgasmic release of sexual tension without first demonstrating color changes of the minor labia.

Orgasm in the human female is just as specific a reaction as it is in the human male. Masters and Johnson call it "an explosive physiological entity" and this explosive quality is the outstanding feature of this process. The sexual tension which has steadily been building up during the earlier phases is now released in a series of violent spasms. These contractions occur at intervals of eight-tenths of a second, just as they do in the male, and they cause the swollen outer part of the vagina to contract strongly from three to fifteen times. These contractions or spasms have given rise to the idea that the vagina grasps the penis at the moment of orgasm and may even refuse to release it, a myth which probably receives reinforcement from observations of the "hanging on" phenomenon in copulating dogs.

The total convulsion involved in female orgasm seems almost as severe as it is in the male. The grimace and contortion of the woman's face graphically expresses the muscular strain which occurs in almost all the major muscles of the body. The muscles of hands and feet, of neck and back, the long muscles of the arms and legs may all undergo powerful spasms. Muscles of the abdomen and buttocks are often contracted intentionally by a sexually aroused woman in the effort to break through from high plateau to orgasmic release.

The uterus also contracts strongly at orgasm, a fact which

has given rise to the idea that the sexually stimulated uterus sucks the semen into itself, thus aiding the process of fertilization. Masters and Johnson, ruthless enemies of sexual myths, have shown that the exact opposite occurs. Far from sucking in the semen the contractions of the uterus at orgasm are such as to ensure that the semen would be expelled if it had entered. The wave of contraction starts at the top of the uterus and works toward its opening into the vagina. It is so powerful that, if orgasm is induced in a woman during menstruation, the menstrual blood can be seen to be forcibly ejected in spurts from the mouth of the uterus. This ejection of the blood and the decongestion it induces explains why many women find orgasm at the height of the menstrual flow relieves the discomfort often associated with this state.

The fact that the uterus, by its muscular contractions, tends to expel rather than draw in the deposited semen makes it seem more than ever remarkable that any human being ever manages to get conceived. Furthermore (another Masters and Johnson discovery) there are vaginas in which a lethal factor exists, capable of immobilizing and killing all sperm in less than a minute. The acidity of the vagina would itself be lethal to the sperm were it not for the fact that semen is strongly buffered and neutralizes the acid. The pH of the vagina goes from 3.5 (very acid) to about 7.0 (neutral) in nine seconds after ejaculation. Even under these conditions, however, all sperm left in the vagina are dead ten hours later.

The heart rate of the human female is affected by the orgasmic explosion just as powerfully as is that of the male. The heart beats rapidly and violently and the blood pressure rises as a result. Breathing becomes very rapid and rates as high as 40 per minute have been observed. The sexual flush envelops more of the body and a filmy sheen of perspiration may appear over the back, thighs and chest.

The female orgasm differs from that of the male in two important respects. First there is nothing in any way equivalent to ejaculation. The lubricating material produced in the vagina does not increase at orgasm. The clitoris, homologue of the penis, does not produce any fluid. Second the female is capable of experiencing a second orgasm very shortly after the first. She does not, as does almost every normal male, pass into a "refractory period" during which detumescence of the penis makes actual copulation impossible. Indeed it is possible for a woman to experience one orgasm after another until physical exhaustion intervenes. Rarely there occurs a condition called *status orgasmus* in which one orgasm follows another so rapidly that the woman remains in continuous orgasm for sixty seconds or longer. This state puts a considerable strain on the woman's body, especially on the heart which beats with furious rapidity as long as the condition continues.

These studies of Masters and Johnson make it clear that the female orgasm, though not directly associated with reproduction as is that of the male, is a physical reality, not some vague figment of the imagination. During the Victorian era, when a fog of hypocrisy enveloped sexual phenomena in the Western world, the belief was encouraged that the female orgasm was a myth, or if not a myth, was certainly unladylike. Even when this fog began to dissipate many obscurities remained, for there certainly were women who rarely or never experienced orgasm. There was, moreover, doubt as to what the female orgasm really was. Did it center around the clitoris or the vagina? Were there two kinds of orgasm, clitoral and vaginal?

These questions have now been answered conclusively. The female orgasm is physically based on a series of contractions of the lower third of the vagina. These are accompanied by contractions of the uterus. The clitoris itself does not undergo any observable changes during orgasm. It is a channel for sexual arousal, though "most women prefer to avoid the overwhelming intensity of sensual focus that may develop from direct clitoral contact." Marriage manuals which advise the male to rouse his partner by directly handling the clitoris are offering counsel of questionable value. Manipulation of the entire area of the *mons veneris,* or even the manipulation of the breasts, is sufficient to induce orgasm in many women but that orgasm, when it occurs, is always centered about the contractions of the vagina. The idea that clitoral and vaginal orgasms are separate entities is a myth.

THE GLANDS AND THE BRAIN

All sexual behavior depends on the activity of two organs, the sex glands and the brain. Without the glands and the hormones they produce there would be no sexual urge. Without the brain there would be no behavior of any kind, for the brain alone coordinates and directs activity. We might think, because male behavior is so different from female behavior, that there is an actual difference in the structure of the male and female brain. This is not so. Inject a male with sufficient female hormone and he will behave as a female. Obviously the sex hormones have power to act on the brain and change behavior entirely. We must now consider the nature of these hormones.

The substances concerned are called androgens and estrogens. All androgens have male hormone activity, estrogens have female hormone activity. There are several androgens and estrogens, some of them natural, some synthetic. The main natural androgen is testosterone, produced by the cells in the testes that lie between the sperm-producing tubules. The main natural estrogen is estradiol, produced in the ovary.

These two substances are very alike (Fig. 22). Indeed, it has been stated by a waggish chemist that the sole difference between Romeo and Juliet was a methyl group and a couple of double bonds. The statement is an oversimplification because it ignores the genetic difference. Romeo's cells contain the XY combination of sex chromosomes; Juliet's the XX. The hormone exerted its influence at a surprisingly early age. As early embryos both Romeo and Juliet had a gonad (sex gland) which was neither a testicle nor an ovary. As they developed,

Romeo's gonad produced testosterone, the action of which resulted in the formation of male genitalia, prostate, seminal vesicles and a penis. Juliet's gonad produced estradiol, which, acting on the same primitive organs, equipped her with ovaries, a uterus, a vagina and a clitoris. This all happened before birth.

After exerting themselves in this fashion the gonads of both the future lovers became dormant, until, roused by the glandular timekeeper at the base of the brain (the front part of the pituitary), they reawakened at the time of puberty and provided Romeo with the sexual equipment of the fully developed male and Juliet with that of the female. The same hormones that produced these changes in the body also generated the powerful urges in the brain which brought the lovers together but which, instead of resulting in normal mating, brought nothing but misery to both parties on account of various obstacles placed by a sexually imbecilic society in the path of healthy development. Of which more later.

Here it suffices to say that the sex hormones in mammals play two roles at different stages of development. First they act on the embryo and determine the pattern of its growth, deciding whether it shall come into the world with the equipment of a male or a female. Second they act again at the time of puberty and determine the kind of sexual behavior the indi-

Testosterone   Estradiol

22. *Male hormone and female hormone.*

vidual shall manifest. That they influence behavior by acting on the brain is obvious. The brain is the origin of behavior. But how they exert their effects is not so obvious. They are, after all, quite simple substances and resemble each other very closely. How can the difference between a mere trace of estradiol and testosterone in the circulating blood have such a fundamental effect on the activity of the organism?

No simple answer can be given to this question. We can say, however, that there are quite specific areas in the brain which absorb the sex hormones from the blood. These centers appear to be stimulated in some way by the hormone and there results a definite pattern of behavior. The sex centers are located at the base of the brain, close to the hypothalamus. When minute amounts of testosterone are injected into this part of the brain in a male rat, strong male activity results. The female also responds with male sexual activity when injected with testosterone. "One heroic female," writes Alan E. Fisher, who performed these experiments, "persisted in malelike behavior over a period of eight weeks in tests conducted every other day." [19]

However, if the testosterone is injected into another area of the brain that lies very close to the sex center it produces entirely different behavior. The male rat becomes maternal! It gathers up scraps of paper and makes a nest. If baby rats are placed in its path it solicitously picks them up and puts them in the nest instead of eating them as would a normal male rat. Behavior therefore depends on what part of the brain the hormone enters. Testosterone, injected into the wrong place, behaves like the hormone progesterone, which it closely resembles. This is a female hormone, the hormone of motherhood, the hormone which prevents the uterus from expelling the embryo until the appropriate time. It is not a sex hormone. It is produced by the ovary in the second part of the female cycle (after ovulation). Continuously produced during pregnancy it inhibits ovulation as long as it dominates the female system. For this reason the celebrated pill, hailed as man's

best weapon against the population explosion, contains substances which have an action like that of progesterone.

Brain injury can drastically alter the manifestations of sex
energy. There are, in the brain, two lobes that hang down
over the ears and are called the temporal lobes. In monkeys,
if both these lobes are surgically removed many changes occur
in the animal's behavior. The monkeys (all of them males),
observed by Dr. H. Klüver and P. C. Bucy, became sex-
obsessed to the point of insanity. "When the monkey is confined alone in a cage, the following states and activities can
be observed: frequent erection of the penis, often without
previous manipulation, the glans penis being clearly visible; or
semi-erection, the animal at times apparently falling asleep
with the penis in the mouth; manipulating or pulling at the
penis or scrotum, even while the animal is standing; 'yawning'
(as seen in copulatory reactions) and, at the same time, manipulation of the genitalia while lying on the back or side; oral
and manual exploration of the genitalia while the animal is in
all kinds of positions, for instance, biting of the penis while
swinging back and forth with the feet suspended from the
top of the cage and with the hands pressed against the hindquarters; long-continued biting of the fingers, toes, feet, legs
and other parts of the body; grabbing the bars of the cage and
pressing the hindquarters rhythmically against them, and 'pre-
senting reactions' on approach of an observer. Grabbing the
finger of the observer may be immediately followed by general
bodily activity and penile erection.

"Whenever other monkeys are put into the same cage, various forms of heterosexual and homosexual behavior can be
observed. The monkey may, for instance, copulate almost continuously for half an hour. It may leave the female only to
mount again immediately. If two bilateral male monkeys are
put together, sexual behavior may take forms which make it
necessary to separate the animals. One of the monkeys while
lying on the seat of the cage may reach with one hand toward
the floor to grab the erect penis of the other monkey and prac-

tically lift the animal from the floor. The animal which is being lifted may do nothing but utter a grunt. Or one monkey may grab the tail of the other and in pulling it across the edge of the seat incidentally break the tail. While one monkey mounts the other and performs copulatory movements, the other one may be seen standing with erect penis. Or both monkeys may lie on the floor and mutually explore each other's genitalia. One monkey may ride on the back of the other and at the same time suck one of its ears. Although they frequently bite each other's legs, arms or tail, fights never develop, and injuries are merely the by-product of heightened sexual activity." [20]

Excessive and abnormal sexual activity was also displayed by male cats in which a part of the brain called the amygdala had been removed. Male cats thus treated mounted not only female cats but also male cats. When four of these "preparations" were placed together each would attempt to mount the other until often as many as four cats were piled up in "tandem copulation," reminiscent of the orgies of the Roman *spintriae*. So unrestricted and undiscriminating was the sexual enthusiasm of these brain-injured cats that they would also attempt copulation with a small, rather friendly dog, a female rhesus monkey, an agouti and an old hen.[21]

All this proves beyond doubt that the normal sexual impulse involves a most delicate balance between brain and glands. Excessive sexual need and great sexual activity can result as much from an injury in certain parts of the brain as from an overactive gland. This is as true of human beings as it is of cats and monkeys, except that the human, the most oversexed of mammals, often behaves like one of the Klüver-Bucy monkeys even without any damage to his temporal lobes.

Sexual behavior thus depends on the action of sex hormones on certain centers of the brain. Even so, it is not always correct to call sexual intercourse an instinctive reaction. It is instinctive, that is to say unlearned, in the forms below the primate level but apes, monkeys and men appear to need education in the art of love. This was demonstrated by the studies of Dr. Harry F. Harlow on the behavior of monkeys raised in isolation without mothers or with dummy mothers of wire netting and terrycloth. Monkeys so raised showed an almost complete absence of sexual know-how. The males would attempt to mount the female's head or approach from the side. Some monkeys, which had been raised in complete isolation to protect them from disease, had virtually no interest in sex at all. "The unhappy beasts sat about morosely, staring vacantly into space now and then, as if in sheer frustration, biting and tearing their own arms and legs."

The evidence suggests that these monkeys learn by watching. The adults copulate, the little ones imitate. There is, in nature, no talk of "lewd and lascivious conduct" or of "undermining the morals of a minor." Sex education is part of the general preparation for living, which includes knowing where to find food and how to avoid foes. Only man, the brainiest of the primates, has managed to become so entangled in his own taboos that he regards practical sex education of the young as immoral when, in fact, it is necessary and important, a natural part of education. Such honest investigations as those of Drs. Masters and Johnson may pave the way for a saner attitude on the part of those responsible for training the young.

SEX ENERGY AND AGING

Sex energy can now be defined as the product of the interaction of the sex hormones and the brain. There are definite sex centers in the brain and they generate sexual urges. But the fire is lit and fueled by the hormones. No hormone, no urge. A burst of hormone production before a baby is born determines the path of development. Give the embryo testosterone, it develops testicles and a penis; give it estradiol and it develops ovaries and a vagina. Then the sex glands become quiescent until reawakened at puberty. The full force of the sex urge engulfs the human male at this time; his greatest sexual need and sexual capacity coincides with adolescence and early manhood (precisely the time at which, in our sexually inept society, he has least opportunity for normal gratification). In the female the urge develops more slowly, reaching a peak in the late twenties or in the thirties.

There follows a gradual decline in the level of sex energy, accepted by some, bitterly resented by others. "Cursed old age," exclaimed the sexual athlete Casanova, "thou art only worthy of dwelling in hell." Frank Harris, another lively lover, envied woman in his old age because woman, the passive sex, could continue to give herself to the end, even on her deathbed if she wished. But man "went about looking like a man, feeling like a man, but powerless, impotent, disgraced in the very pride and purpose of his manhood." [22] These lamentations, of course, represent only one side of the picture. There are many who find it a relief to be free of sexual desire, as was Sophocles who, asked when an old man if he still indulged in the pleasures of sexual love, exclaimed: "Heaven forbid! I have fled from them as from a harsh and cruel tyrant."

Whether a man's reaction to the decline of sex energy resembles that of Casanova or Sophocles there can be no doubt about the reality of this decline. Both in the male and in the female, production of the sex hormones falls off in later life. The decline is most abrupt in the female. The menopause or climacteric takes place when a woman's ovary runs out of eggs. When the ovary runs out of eggs and ceases to function, the female body is deprived of those hormones it previously produced. This results in several changes, both in the appearance of the body and its functioning. "As the fifty-year road marker is passed," writes Dr. William H. Masters, "the female runs a well-charted course. The breasts lose tone and sag. The mons flattens and loses body. The vaginal mucosa becomes thin and atropic with the disappearance of its rugal pattern. The cervix and corpus shrink to their prepubertal status and ratio. The ovaries are shrunken in size, have granular serosal coats and are obviously nonfunctioning." [23]

Many women pass through the menopause without discomfort. Others are plagued by hot flashes, waves of heat traveling over the body accompanied by a flush and often profuse perspiration. Dizziness, fatigue and a sense of weakness may be experienced. Depression is sometimes profound and may become incapacitating, a condition known as involutional melancholia. So the climacteric is apt to be a time of difficulty and readjustment during which the chemistry of the body changes over from one pattern to a different pattern.

As the hormones which the ovaries manufacture can be made synthetically and are fairly cheap it seems logical that the aging female should receive the benefit of these substances which her own ovaries can no longer make. Such hormone therapy will render more comfortable her transition into what Dr. Masters has called "the third sex." There is, of course, really no third sex, but those individuals, both male and female, in whom the sex glands have finally failed might be thought of as belonging to a neutral gender. Disappearance of the sex urge may not seem much of a hardship to many women, and the loss of the ability to become pregnant may be welcomed. But failure of sex-hormone production may have other results, such as wasting of the muscles and loss of calcium from the bones which may interfere with the enjoyment of life. In the opinion of many students of aging these unpleasant aspects of physical senility could be avoided by properly balanced administration of sex hormones. Dr. Masters is of this opinion and finds fault with the practicing physician for failing to make use of these substances sufficiently often or sufficiently soon.

"One of the tragedies of modern medicine is that, while we now have the weapons with which to rescue the early senile individual from, or at least to delay the onset of, the obvious consequences of his 'disease,' we do little or nothing to prevent the development of this clinical state."

There are several reasons why the average practicing physician hesitates to use sex-hormone replacement therapy. To begin with, there are many sex hormones. Besides the natural ones, testosterone and alpha estradiol, there are a lot of synthetic ones. Some are weak. Others are very potent but produce undesirable side effects. They may cause the body to retain more fluid than it should. There is also a suspicion that testosterone may rouse the fires of certain forms of cancer if these fires are already smoldering in the body.

Then there is the injection problem. The most potent hormones are effective only when injected or implanted under the skin and many elderly people object to having their buttocks used as pincushions or to having little tunnels bored in their persons for the purpose of holding hormone pellets. So, if hormone replacement therapy is to be a long-term affair, it becomes more or less essential to discover hormones which can be taken by mouth. Such hormones are available, but those known at present are somewhat low in potency.

Administration of estrogens to women at the menopause may have an additional undesirable effect of causing bleeding from the uterus. This can be prevented, according to Masters, by administering the estrogen in combination with an androgen such as testosterone. The ratio of androgen to estrogen is important. Too much estrogen and a woman will start to bleed. Too much androgen and she will start growing a moustache and develop a low gruff voice like that of a sergeant major. In short she will become masculinized, as is only to be expected when her body is full of male hormone. Dr. Masters advocated a ratio of twenty parts androgen to one of estrogen and observed considerable improvement in the health of the elderly females to whom such balanced medication was given.

According to Masters and Johnson some women react to the menopause in a positive, others in a negative fashion. As the menses terminate, the freedom from fear of pregnancy may result in an upsurge of sexual interest. For this reason many women experience a "second honeymoon" during their early fifties. The exhausting demands imposed by the duty of raising a family have ceased in most cases when a woman reaches this age. New directions are sought as outlets for unexpended physical energy and reawakened mental activity. If these unused energies flow in sexual channels they may initiate a hunt for new sexual partners or for variations on familiar and unsatisfying sexual routines.

Other women react to the menopause in the opposite way. They close the gates with a sense of relief and write *Finis* to their love lives. Such women have often derived little satisfaction from sexual activity at the best of times. Their performance has been inadequate, their sexual tensions unresolved, they have been unlucky in their choice of sexual partners. They may also be influenced by the Victorian concept that it is not ladylike for an older woman to be interested in sexual activity.

Apart from all this, Masters and Johnson have shown that the act of coitus is often unrewarding for women past the menopause. The thinning of the vaginal walls and inadequacy of lubrication may make penetration difficult. The uterine contractions which form a normal part of the female orgasm may become painful. This uterine pain is evidently due to "steroid starvation," because it can be eliminated by suitable combinations of estrogen and progesterone. Apart from these direct obstacles to sexual pleasure any woman is apt to become relatively asexual when experiencing such menopausal discomforts as fatigue, flushing, nervousness, emotional irritability, headaches and vague pains in the pelvic region.

The male fares, as far as his hormones go, somewhat better than the female. His testes continue to function into old age, but their hormone production becomes increasingly inadequate. He suffers from hormone starvation which affects not only his level of sex energy but also the strength of his muscles, for the sex hormone does far more than arouse sexual desire. It influences the rate at which protein is built up by the body. One who is short of testosterone tends to use up his own muscles: he goes, as the saying is, into negative nitrogen balance, breaking down his own protein faster than he makes it.

"There is no question of the fact that the human male's sexual responsiveness wanes as he ages." Masters and Johnson have described the way in which it wanes. The entire act is toned down, muted, transferred to a lower key. Frequency of intercourse, intensity of sensation, speed of attaining erection, force of ejaculation all are reduced. Whereas the young male may shoot his semen fully two feet, the old one dribbles it out a mere six inches. Only in one respect does age bring improvement in male sexual performance. The elderly male, once erection is attained, can maintain it without reaching orgasm for a longer time than can the younger male. He does this, evidently, because the sensations he receives have been so blunted by the aging process that excitement mounts gradually. Indeed it may frequently happen that the aging male cannot reach the level of excitement at which orgasm occurs. He has the sense of urgency that accompanies the approach of the climax but the force which trips the switch and releases the tension cannot be generated.

The male, like the female, suffers from sex-hormone starvation and the lack of sexual vigor he displays is due, at least in part, to a lack of testosterone. So, when the male sex hormone was discovered and a form of this hormone was synthesized (methyl testosterone) that could be taken by mouth instead of being inserted as a pellet under the skin there seemed nothing to prevent the aging male from taking a new lease of life. No one greeted this prospect more enthusiastically than did Paul de Kruif who devoted a whole book to the description of the discovery and effects of the male hormone. He not only recommended it to others but also took it himself, regarding it as sensible for the aging male to take testosterone as for a diabetic to take insulin.

"So, no different than a good diabetic child who knows that insulin every day makes the difference between living and dying, I'll be faithful and remember to take my twenty or thirty milligrams a day of testosterone. I'm not ashamed that it's no longer made to its old degree by my own aging body. It's chemical crutches. It's borrowed manhood. It's borrowed time. But, just the same, it's what makes bulls bulls. And, who knows, maybe tomorrow they'll hit on a simple dietary trick that will, to a degree, bring back the power of the glands that make my own natural hormone.

"Meanwhile I'll keep taking the methyl testosterone that now gives me the total vitality to go on working and waiting for such a not impossible discovery. Here's hoping." [24]

Were De Kruif's hopes fulfilled? We do not know. What we do know is that hormone replacement therapy (as this treatment is referred to in medical circles) is not always successful. Masters and Johnson are guarded in their comments. "There has been some evidence of reawakened sexual interest subsequent to effective steroid replacement in aging males. Clinical impression suggests that the obvious elevation of eroticism is not a direct effect of steroid replacement. Rather it may be a secondary result of the obvious improvement in total body economy and of a renewed sense of wellbeing."

In other words sex hormone prevents the aging male from using up his protein faster than he can replace it. It keeps him in "positive protein balance." Its effect on sexuality is secondary.

SEXUAL BOREDOM

One of the main reasons for a decline in sexual performance of the aging male is boredom with his mate. This is described by Masters and Johnson as "probably the most constant factor in the loss of aging male's interest in sexual performance with his partner." One is reminded of Lawrence Durrell's description of "the disgusted and dispirited faces of the long-married, tied to each other back to back, so to speak, like dogs unable to disengage after coupling." [25] One thinks of Kipling's comparison of a woman and a cigar:

Maggie my wife at fifty—grey and dour and old—
With never another Maggie to purchase for love or gold!
And the light of the Days that have Been, the dark of the Days that
    Are,
And Love's torch stinking and stale, like the butt of a dead cigar—
The butt of a dead cigar you are bound to keep in your pocket
With never a new one to light though it's burnt and charred to the
    socket.

The lamentations of the Micronesians, victims of interfering American administrators who put a stop to the long-established custom of elderly men taking young concubines, are also instructive. "Older men often comment today that without young women to excite them and without the variety once provided by changing concubines, they have become sexually inactive long before their time. To them a wife is sexually exciting only for a few years after marriage." [26]

Nor is it only the human male who suffers from the emasculating effect of sexual boredom. Male monkeys that had wearied of their partners to the extent of being scarcely able to reach ejaculation perked up promptly and ejaculated speedily as soon as a different female was made available.[27] Bulls, buffalo, sheep and swine all show an enhancement of sexual performance when the number of females available to them is increased. The human male, in this respect, is no different from many other mammals but, held in the fetters of monogamy, is frequently unable to obtain that sexual variety which his nature demands. Consequently sexual performance fails before it need, for Masters and Johnson emphasize that the maintainance of effective sexuality in the aging male depends on his level of sexual activity. Unused organs atrophy. The sex organs are no exception. However, all is not lost, even when sexual inadequacy has become established. ". . . the male

over fifty years old can be trained out of his secondarily acquired impotence in a high percentage of cases."

Craving for a new partner, the elderly male dreams of
young girls, hoping to absorb from their bodies some vitalizing
elixir. Inhalation of the breath of young girls was a method
used by the ancients in quest of rejuvenation, as we learn from
an inscription on an ancient grave: "To Aesculapius and
Health—L. Claudius Hermip—who lived one hundred and fifteen years and five days with the aid of the breath of young
women, to the surprise of physicians. Lead your life accordingly." King David's deathbed experiment with the virgin
Abishag was evidently intended to involve copulation rather
than inhalation but "he knew her not" and died soon after-
ward.

The craving of the elderly male for the very young female is
not necessarily confined to the human species. We have this
on the authority of Frank Harris. After confessing that in his
later years "desire became rampant in me only at the sight of
slight half-fledged girlhood" (Nabokov's nymphets) he goes
on to relate the following curious adventure:

"While living in Roehampton and editing the *Saturday Review*, I used to ride nearly every day in Richmond Park. One
morning I noticed something move in the high bracken, and
riding to the spot, found a keeper kneeling beside a young
doe. 'What's the matter?' I asked.

"'Matter enough,' he replied, holding up the two hind legs
of the little creature, showing me that they were both broken.

"'Here she is, Sir,' he went on. 'As pretty as a picture, ain't
she? Just over a year or so old, the poor little bitch, and she
come in heat this autumn and she must go and pick out the
biggest and oldest stag in the park and rub her little bottom
against him—Didn't you, you poor little bitch!—and of course
he mounted her, Sir; and her two little sticks of legs snapped
under his weight and I found her lying broken without ever
had any pleasure; and now I've got to put her out of her pain,

Sir; and she's so smooth and pretty! Aint ye?' And he rubbed his hand caressingly along her silky fur.

" 'Must you kill her?' I asked, 'I'd pay to have her legs set.'

" 'No, no,' he replied, 'It would take too much time and trouble and there's many of them. Poor little bitch must die,' and as he stroked her fine head gently, the doe looked up at him with her big eyes drowned in tears.

" 'Do you really lose many in that way?' I asked.

" 'Not so many, Sir,' he replied. 'If she had got over this season she'd have been strong enough next year to have borne the biggest. It was just her bad luck,' he said, 'to have been born in the troop of the oldest and heaviest stag in the park.'

" 'Has age anything to do with the attraction?' I asked.

" 'Surely it has,' replied the keeper. 'The old stag is always after these little ones, and young does are always willing. I guess it's animal nature,' he added, as if regretfully.

" 'Animal nature,' I said to myself as I rode away, 'and human nature as well, I fear,' with heavy apprehension or presentiment compressing my heart." [22]

III.
SEX ENERGY
DEIFIED

THE DEIFIED PHALLUS

THE FIRST PART of this book dealt with the manifestations of sex energy in nature. In it we see an incredibly powerful force showing itself in varied and sometimes sinister forms, ranging from the complex hermaphrodite embrace of the snail to the cannibalistic love feast of the praying mantis. In man the manifestations of sex energy have become even more elaborate. This large-brained, unharmonious hominid, the only member of the primate stock that habitually eats meat and systematically murders large numbers of members of his own species, is almost insanely sexual as compared with the majority of mammals. Every season is his mating season. The female is always in heat, the male always ready. Moreover this unbalanced creature, whose instinctive brain has fallen under the dominance of his overgrown cerebral cortex, cannot simply accept his sexual impulses and satisfy them in a normal healthy manner. He is, instead, forever either glorifying them or degrading them. The history of man's interference with his own sexual impulse is so complicated that its description requires several chapters.

We begin with the story of the worship of the phallus. We may assume, on the basis of Neolithic art, that man has long been fascinated by his own penis. Its extraordinary capacity for erection, its independence, its strength when fully engorged and the voluptuous sensations it is capable of generating set it apart from other organs of the body. Thus the phallus early became an object of worship and remained one for many centuries, nor was this worship confined to barbaric races to whom we might justly apply the term primitive. No capital in the ancient world was more sophisticated than the Alexandria of Ptolemy Philadelphus. It was the very center of the arts and sciences, its museum a treasure house whose glories surpassed those of Athens. Yet it was Ptolemy, a most enlightened monarch (he was patron of the seventy scholars who first translated the Old Testament into Greek), who caused to be carried through the streets in a religious procession an enormous representation of the male organ one hundred and twenty cubits long. The populace neither jeered nor sniggered. They greeted the prodigy with reverence and several poets composed odes in its honor.

In Heiropolis in ancient Syria the phallus was also enthusiastically worshipped. At the gate of the temple of Priapic Diana stood a phallus so enormous that a priest could ascend to the top of the gigantic organ and remain perched there for seven days enjoying intimate communication with the deity. That Syrian phallus was an object of the most sacred significance, a portion of the symbolism of a complex cult that gave cosmic meaning to both the male and the female sex organs. The phallus was nothing less than the creative power that moves the universe, the force that impregnates the heavens, the earth and the waters. Nor was the phallus alone considered worthy of worship, for what is the value of the male organ without its female counterpart? The ancients, wiser in their way than their contemporary descendants, saw the cosmic creative force as androgynous. Such, Lucian informs us, was the significance of the Priapic Diana. SHE, borne up by bulls, was the passive power of nature, the primordial matter, *prakriti*, the cosmic female. HE, erect and turgid, was the active power, the universal *purusha*, energy, the cosmic male. Between the two fluttered a dove, third member of the triad, proceeding from and consubstantial with both.

Here was a most profound mystery, a cosmic interplay of forces partaking in the drama of creation. In this drama the universal phallus was thought of as playing a part analogous to its role in sexual intercourse. The suggestion that there was anything indecent about such a representation would have seemed to the ancients impious in the extreme. Only small and polluted minds would entertain such a thought.

The deification of the sexual organs was by no means confined to Heiropolis and Alexandria. All over the ancient world, from the banks of the Ganges to the plains of Roman Britain, we find this pattern of worship. Let us take as a typical example Varro's account of the phallic procession in Lanuvium. It occurred in the spring, the season of growth and renewal, the time reserved for the adoration of Father Liber, a Romanized version of Bacchus or Dionysus. The symbol of the god Liber, a phallus crimson in color and generous in size, was taken from its shrine amid public rejoicings. The gaudy organ, handled with the reverence due to so potent a deity, was propped in an erect position in a gaily decorated wagon. Pulled by a yoke of white oxen wreathed in garlands of early flowers, the wagon made its way through the city gates, through fields green with the promise of harvest, through orchards white with blossom and vineyards on whose vines the buds were bursting.

For a whole month the citizens of Lanuvium continued their celebrations, praising the effigy, organ of outflow and generation, symbol of the friendliness of the deity toward his creations. Before it was finally restored to its shrine the most virtuous matrons of the town publically crowned with wreaths the symbol of that force on which their hope for offspring depended. Then the phallus was returned to its shrine until the following spring.

There was no false shame here, no hypocrisy in the face of biological realities. As the vine, sacred to Bacchus, sent forth shoots stiffened with the turgor of the rising sap, so the virile member of the male, similarly stiffened, throbbed with the identical generative power, the joyous, juice-squirting Dionysian frenzy which not only regenerated but also liberated, giving to man a taste of ecstasy, bringing him into direct contact with the divine.

"The procreative miracle," wrote Rattray Taylor in *Sex in History*, "was the ever repeated proof of the existence of God, and the sign that his aim and nature was to create life and to dispel the force of darkness, decay and death. It was the one solid reason for optimism in a world which must have seemed to them as dangerous and destructive as our own. They approached this recurrent demonstration of God's bounty and goodwill with holy awe and, like Corinthus, who replied to the Father's horror of the phallic by saying that man should not be ashamed of what God has not been ashamed to create, they carried in religious procession symbols of the phallus and pudenda in all innocence, and called the sexual parts *aidos* or *aidion*—that which inspires holy awe." [28]

In Rome the worship of the phallus took a most direct and practical form. There, in the early days, the phallic god, under his Roman aspect Mutunus Tutunus, received the virginities of prospective brides who reverently deflowered themselves on his wooden or ivory member. It did not seem in the least indecent to the girl to sacrifice her virginity in this manner. On the contrary, it was a profound religious experience. By uniting with the god she partook of a sacred mystery, received a taste of maleness in its totality. By her communion with the divine principle she was rendered fruitful and better able to fulfil her wifely duties. In gratitude for benefits received, the girl offered on the altar of the god small phallic images the number of which equaled the number of men who had acted as priests on the occasion of her initiation. We still possess an ancient poem in which a young lady called Lalage presents to the deity the pictures of the *Elephantis* (a monograph on sexual postures) and gravely requests that she may enjoy the pleasures over which he particularly presides in all the postures described in that celebrated thesis. She expressed these sentiments in the gravest and most perfectly devout spirit, without a thought of indecency or impropriety. If she did this nowadays she would probably be arrested as a "juvenile delinquent."

Among several peoples in the ancient world the active force of generation was symbolized by some animal. The serpent, at Cos or Epidaurus, linked with the cult of Aesculapius about whose staff it coiled, symbolized primarily the healing power. But the healing power, or power of *regeneration,* was but an aspect of the power of generation which had created living things in the first place. So the serpent, whose form suggested that of the male organ, became the symbol of sexual as well as of healing power.

In this animal symbolism were blended several different forms. A celebrated bronze in the Vatican has the male organ of generation placed on the head of a cock, emblem of the sun, supported on the neck and shoulders of a man. This composition, says Richard Payne Knight in his "Discourse on the Worship of Priapus," [29] represented the generative power of Eros, Osiris, Mithras or Bacchus, whose center is the sun, incarnate in man. On the pedestal of the bronze was the inscription "The Savior of the World."

The animal symbolism employed by the ancient Egyptians seemed curious to Herodotus. At Mendes, the Greek historian informs us, a living goat was employed as an image of the generative power. To this deity women presented themselves naked and considered it an honor to be sexually enjoyed by the god. To moderns such a performance would seem obscene, worthy of shady nightclubs which stage perverse displays to titillate the jaded appetites of their patrons. To the Egyptians, however, the act represented the incarnation of the deity and the communication of his creative spirit to man. Says Knight: "It was one of the sacraments of that ancient church and was, without doubt, beheld with that pious awe and reverence with which devout persons always contemplate the mysteries of their faith, whatever they happen to be."

In addtion to the serpent and the goat the bull was widely worshipped. As a symbol of the active male principle this powerful beast was a logical choice. To emphasize the connection with sexual force the head of a bull (in amulets designed to be worn about the neck) was often embellished with two male organs. This represented not only the strength of the creator but also the direction of the power, its application to the most beneficent of purposes, the propagation of sensitive beings.

With the extension of the Roman Empire the worship of the generative organs became exceedingly widespread. Though prudes have conspired to hide them from the public eye an incredible number of phallic amulets lie moldering in secret drawers in various museums. In Roman cities the phallus was everywhere. It confronted the traveler from the moment he entered the gates. "A phallus," wrote Kiefer in *Sexual Life in Ancient Rome*, "was sometimes set up above city gates as a protection against ill luck. Sometimes under such a phallus appears the inscription: *Hic Habitat Felicitas*—happiness dwells here. This of course does not mean that the place guaranteed any sort of sexual happiness, only that the phallus expelled unhappiness by its magic." [30] It was on account of its magical power that the phallus, in the form of the *fascinum*, was suspended about the necks of children. By attracting the glance of stray beholders it was thought to be capable of averting the evil eye. From this aspect of the phallus cult are derived our words "fascinate" and "fascination."

In France of Roman times the cult developed its most exotic forms. The center of the cult was in Nemausus, which is now the city of Nîmes. In one astonishing piece of sculpture, illustrated in Thomas Wright's "The Worship of the Generative Powers," [31] is displayed a triple phallic beast, which possesses, in addition to a phallus and testicles in the usual place, a rampant phallus forming the head and a wrinkled phallus forming the tail (Fig. 23). The smallest phallus is adorned with a bell, the large head phallus has sprouted a pair of wings and the whole beast is carried on the legs of a goat. Standing next to this prodigy, correctly dressed according to the fashion of the times, is a Roman matron restraining on a leash with raised right hand the rampaging head phallus which is fully a head taller than she, while with pendant left, in a thong like a sling, she holds up the wrinkled tail phallus which must otherwise trail in the dust.

Concerning this curious beast a learned French antiquary has speculated as follows: "Perhaps it signifies the empire of woman extending over the three ages of man; on youth characterized by the bell; on the age of vigor, the ardor of which she restrains; and on old age which she sustains."

In Britain as in France the phallic cult was so popular as to convince archaeologists of a less liberal age that their ancestors were either very dirty-minded or obsessed with sex to the point of being psychopathic. The triple phallic beast, worn in the form of a pendant or as earrings, appears to have been greatly in demand. Two such beasts are illustrated in Knight's book, delightful creatures dancing with priapic vigor, with the legs of dogs, wings on the principal phallus and loops to

23. The triple phallic beast of Nemausus. "Perhaps it signifies the empire of woman extending over the three ages of man."

which bells were originally attached, supplementary symbols whose concavity suggested the female organ (Fig. 24).

24. Phallic amulets from Roman Britain.

A PHALLIC ODYSSEUS

For moderns still living under the shadow of the Judeo-Christian guilt cult which, though much weakened, still distorts our thinking and feeling, it is useful to try to reenter the climate of ideas of the ancient world in which sex energy was worshipped as a manifestation of the divine.

This reentry is made easier by the fact that one of the great novels of antiquity, the *Satyricon* of Petronius, deals with the adventures of a man who has offended the sexual god, Priapus. This god was sometimes represented as a phallus and little else; alternately he took the form of a grotesque little man with both arms upraised and a huge organ of generation upraised also. He was a god of vegetation, closely related to Pan, protecting and aiding the sexual processes of nature.

It is to William Arrowsmith, whose lively and unexpurgated translation of the book is probably the best available,[32] that we owe the idea of the Phallic Odysseus. "The whole work could be (and has been) described as a kind of burlesque or mock-epic, an *Odyssey buffa* or satyr's *Aeneid*, in which Encolpius, like an anti-hero, suffers the wrath of an outraged Priapus . . . Just as Odysseus suffered the wrath of Poseidon and was driven over land and sea to learn the customs of men and their ways so here Encolpius (his name means roughly 'the Crotch') is persecuted by the heavy anger of the lord of lust, Priapus." In the first century A.D. when Nero occupied the throne of the Caesars, the citizens were so deity-ridden that, as Quartilla put it in the *Satyricon*, "one might meet a god more easily than a man." With so many gods available even the process of attaining an erection was under divine control. It was Priapus who managed this particular department of human physiology and it was this god that Encolpius offended by inadvertently witnessing the secret rites in the grotto of Priapus.

One thing the gods of the ancient world could not tolerate was the profanation of their mysteries. The Roman authorities took a serious view of the matter also, and such profanations were punishable with death. "No man on earth may look on forbidden things as you have done and escape unpunished . . . I am afraid that in your youthful indiscretion you may be led to reveal the things you saw in the chapel of Priapus and divulge our mysteries to the world. And so I kneel before you now with outstretched hands and I beg you, I beseech you, not to make a mockery of our nocturnal rites or reveal a secret so jealously guarded over the centuries, a secret which scarcely a thousand men have ever known."

Though Encolpius was forgiven by the priestess of Priapus he was not let off so lightly by the deity. Time and again the unfortunate young man was afflicted, at the critical moment, with that humiliating condition that contemporary sexologists have termed psychogenic impotence. Even Circe, the beautiful courtesan, could not rouse him to the necessary state of turgor.

"At this I went purple with shame, completely losing even what little strength I had left. I felt as though my whole body had suddenly wilted away. "For god's sake," I begged her, "take pity on my misery. Don't mock me. I must be under a spell. Someone must have cursed me . . ."

Furious over his failure the wretched Encolpius threatened his penis with a razor but was foiled by the extreme contraction of the part involved.

> Three times with razor raised I tried to lop;
> three times my trembling fingers let it drop,
> while he, as limp as cabbage when it's boiled,
>   with prickish fright my purpose foiled.
>
> For, cold as ice, he shrank, too scared to watch,
> and screwed his crinkled length against my crotch,
> so cramped along my gut, so furled and small,
>   I could not see to cut at all.

Baffled, I mused: how bring the blade to bear?
How lop that thing so wee it seemed not there
at all? But wait, I thought: if steel won't kill,
    perhaps my verbal engines will.

Thereupon he roundly upbraided his penis calling it the shame of gods and man, an "obscene, unspeakable sullen pendant," which had fixed upon his youth, his green and swelling years, the scandal of decrepit, limp old age. The penis was unmoved and Encolpius filled with shame to find himself engaged in such a ridiculous argument with "a part of me which no serious man thinks worthy of his thoughts." But after all why not? Do not men curse their guts, their teeth, their heads. Didn't Ulysses himself have a parley with his heart? Why should the penis not be considered worthy of being addressed? This thought evoked from the author a statement on the subject of prudery (of which, in old Rome, the crusty Cato was the symbol as Mrs. Grundy is in our society) so modern in tone that it has been reproduced here. It is typical of the irritation produced in honest writers from Petronius in the first century to Frank Harris and Henry Miller in the twentieth by those who insist that there is something inherently indecent about sexual manifestations.

    Then why in heaven's name
    must every nagging prude
    of Cato's ilk cry shame,
    denounce my work as lewd,
    damning with a look
    my guileless, simple art,
    this simple, modern book?
    to prudes I now assert
    my purity of speech;
    such candor in my pen
    as will not stoop to teach.
    I write of living men,
    the things they say and do,

of every human act
admitted to be true.
Then where's the shame in that,
if loving men enjoy
the pleasures of the night
whereby each girl and boy
experience delight?
Let prudes in need of proof
heed what Epicurus said,
old master of the truth,
who held that all are led
by their senses to the goal,
life-perfecting Pleasure,
Pleasure is the goal of all,
omnis vitaeque perfector.

Nothing is falser than people's preconceptions and ready-made opinions, nothing is sillier than their sham morality . . .

Finally Encolpius arrived at a shrine of Priapus presided over by two ancient priestesses, Proselenos and Oenothea. There he addressed to the deity a moving prayer, meanwhile keeping an anxious eye cocked to see "if that poor dead part of me would raise its fallen head."

Comrade of Bacchus and the nymphs, you whom lovely Dione
set as god upon our woodlands in their glory;
O lord of Lesbos, god of Thasos' holy green,
whom Lydis, the seven-streamed, adores beside Hypaepa,
O mentor of Bacchus, come!
    Hear me, dryad-lover,
welcome this humble prayer.
    Innocent of harm,
pure in heart, with pious hands, I come to you:
a poor man, in impotence and need, by weakness worn.
I sinned, O lord, yet sinned in part: not all of me
offended. Weakness was my crime, the thing I did not,
could not, do; and being such, was less than crime.
I implore you, lord, purge my tortured soul of guilt;
forgive my petty crime.

        And when once more I see
good fortune laugh, then shall you have the gifts
your deity deserves.
        To your shrine shall go
the ram, the father of the flocks, in horned glory;
to you the squealing sow shall lead her suckling young.
and this year's wine shall froth in bowls for you,
and round about your shrine three times shall dance
the randy, drunken lads in praise, O god, of you.

Even this was not effective and evoked from the priestess Proselenos the following comment:

"Oenothea, this poor miserable creature was born under an unlucky star. Right now there's not a girl or boy in the whole world who'd take his goods at any price. Yes, you've never seen such a wretched thing. Why he's limp as wet leather; there's nothing there at all. Just to show you, what would you think of a man who could get out of bed with Circe without having been satisfied?"

Oenothea, however, knew a remedy. "All I require is that you agree to spend one night here in bed with me, and if I don't make you stand up stiffer than a bull's horn, my name's not Oenothea." Her technique was drastic. She "brought out a leather phallus which she rubbed with a mixture of oil, pepper and ground nettle seed and then slowly inserted into my rectum. Pitilessly sprinkling my thigh with the same mixture, the old hag . . . mixed the juice of watercress with god knows what exotic herb, spattered my penis with the stuff and brushed the lower part of my abdomen with a branch of green nettles . . ."

Whether the treatment worked we do not know, for the document is fragmentary at this point. In any case Priapus finally relented and Encolpius was restored.

"'There are other gods still more powerful,' I explained, 'and it is they who have made me a man once more. Mercury himself, the god who guides our unborn souls to the light and leads the dead to hell, has taken pity on me and given me back that power which an angry hand once cut away. Look at me and tell me whether Protesilaus or any of those ancient heroes was ever more blessed by heaven than I am now.' With that, I lifted my tunic and displayed myself in my erected glory. Gaping with astonishment and awe, utterly incapable of believing his eyes, he reached out his shaking hands and caressed that huge pledge of heaven's favor . . ."

DECLINE AND FALL

The decline and fall of the deified phallus roughly paralleled the decline and fall of the Roman Empire. Even in the work of Petronius we seem to detect a note of mockery as if Priapus, the phallic god, was regarded as comical rather than awe-inspiring. In any case a change occurred and the phallus, in the eyes of Western man, ceased to be venerated as a symbol of god's bounty and came to be regarded instead as the very acme of obscenity. Knight suggests that the phallus started on the downhill path when the god Priapus lost his universal cosmic significance and was turned into little more than a scarecrow, a grotesque figure to be set up in the garden with its enormous phallus painted crimson to frighten birds and thieves. By the time of Augustine, Bishop of Hippo (fifth century A.D.), the phallus was already regarded with disfavor. Augustine expressed nothing but contempt for those bucolic rites that so excited the simple rustics of Lanuvium. He called the object they worshipped "that shameful part of the body" and dubbed the painted phallus they carted through the fields a "disgraceful effigy." These scoldings sounded the keynote for countless other churchmen who set themselves up to criticize the works of their creator and seemed to see nothing irreverent in so doing.

Despite the efforts of various monastics the phallus retained its aura of magic for a remarkably long period. Thus, in a letter written by Sir William Hamilton, dated December 30, 1781, we read that "*ex-voti* of wax, representing the male parts of generation, of various dimensions, some even of the length of the palm" were being publicly offered for sale in the town of Isernia in the kingdom of Naples. The pagan phallus had assumed a Christian disguise. Its waxen image was sold to the devout in the names of Saint Cosmas and Saint Damian. The oil of St. Cosmas was also in high repute for its invigorating qualities and was applied to the organs of generation by the reverend canon in the presence of the awed congregation: *Per intercessionem beati Cosmi, liberet te ab omni malo. Amen.* On such operations, in the year 1780 alone, were expended fourteen thousand flasks of oil!

That Saints Cosmas and Damian managed to retain for the phallus its sacred symbolism through all those dreary centuries of persecution and prudery was a feat worthy of wonder and admiration. Unfortunately for the simple people of Isernia, a new road built to render the town more accessible resulted in its quaint customs becoming known to the world. The revelation provoked shocked comments from Catholics and derisive howls from the Protestants who took these phallic preoccupations as offering fresh proof of the "similitude of the Popish and Pagan religion." So the rites were suppressed.

Only in one other form did the veneration of the virile symbol survive. The Floralia, feast of spring, celebrated by the Romans with sexual orgies and midnight performances by naked actresses in the theaters, was taken over by the Church along with other pagan festivals and converted into a sober, asexual Easter. One old practice slipped past the ecclesiastical censors, that of baking from the finest flour cakes in the form of the phallus or the female sex organ. The practice continued in France until recent times. At St. Jean-d'Angély such phallic cakes were called *fateaux* and were carried in the procession of Corpus Christi. Similar cakes were made in the lower Limousin, especially at Brives, while cookies in the form of the female sex organ were made at Clermont in Auvergne and were popularly called *miches*. But the cold Princes of the

Church finally put a stop to these phallic frolics. The sexy goodies, male and female, were metamorphosed into dull, sexually neutral, hot cross buns.

The degradation of sex energy proceeded in the West until Eros and Aphrodite were buried in a coating of slime and Priapus bowed his phallic head in shame. A maleficent dualism that separated from the flesh a mysterious and ill-defined entity called the spirit split the very nature of man into two warring parts, designating one the higher and the other the lower. Eros was divorced from Agape. Love became twofold, sacred or profane. The ardent embraces of male and female as well as the biological forces that led to such embraces were placed in the profane category. It was admitted, albeit reluctantly, by those who regarded themselves as mankind's spiritual guides that men and women had to unite in this way if the human race was not to become extinct. They insisted, however, that those who indulged in this activity did so at their peril. The whole region of the body involved in the sexual process came to be regarded not as the dwelling place of a god but as the abode of the devil, a dark, hot, evil, sulfurous pit from which emanated a fog of unspeakable temptation. Of this, more later.

FEMALE SEX WORSHIP

Worship of the female sex organ has never been quite as popular as the worship of the phallus. It is so tucked away in the depths of the body that primitive man had only a vague idea of its shape. The external opening of the female sex organ was represented along with the phallus in several of those curious sculptures found at Nîmes. The representation was never entirely satisfactory, indeed, without receiving explanation as to the meaning of these oval forms with slits in the middle, the observer might fail to find in them any sexual significance. (The horseshoe, used as a lucky omen, is also a symbol of the female sex organ though few who hang it over the door recognize it as such.) Far more explicit were the Sheela-na-gig figures found in certain ancient churches in which the symbolic oval was held by a crude representation of a woman in a position approximating the one it occupies in nature.

In the East, in India specifically, the representation of the female sex organ (*yoni*) became even more stylized. It was often represented in union with the male organ (*lingam*) but the profusion of gods, goddesses, serpents, demons and other items of flora and fauna make it hard for the uninitiated to distinguish the sexual symbols from the decorations that surround them.

Far more widespread than the worship of the female sex organ was the worship of woman herself, the Great Mother, the universal giver of life. Among the Babylonians the worship of Ishtar and Astaroth was conducted with an orgiastic enthusiasm. Priestesses of these deities, the Hierodules and Consecrated Women, gave themselves to all comers who could afford to purchase their embraces. A mean and warped morality has dubbed these women temple prostitutes, but for the priestesses no element of prostitution was involved. The act of sexual union was a mode of worship and the money they received went to the temple.

The ancient Minoans, a joyful, vigorous and sexually uninhibited race, were woman-worshippers. Concerning the details of the cult we know very little, for the literature of Minos has not proved revealing. The ivory snake goddess embellished in gold was probably a representation of the great Earth Mother, worshipped in the Cave of Psychro high in the mountains of eastern Crete. One wonders what was the significance of the sport of "bull leaping," indulged in by the Cretan girls. Was it a religious ritual, a demonstration of the superiority of female skill over the brute force of the male? We cannot tell. We know only that woman in ancient Crete led a free and healthy life and that worship of the female principle was probably the dominant religion.

Worship of the goddess of love, the foam-born Aphrodite, attained great popularity throughout the ancient world. Aphrodite gave to the Greeks the delights of love and of beauty, for love and beauty were intertwined and they worshipped both. It was in her honor that the most splendid, popular and dissolute celebrations were performed. Aphrodite was the goddess of spring, the bringer of flowers. She walked entwined in roses and myrtles among woods perfumed with fresh blossom and vibrant with bird song. In Cyprus, where the goddess had been born on the beach at Paphos, the most famous and luxurious of her ceremonies took place. The image of the goddess was bathed in the sea by girls who subsequently bathed themselves, in preparation for the coming orgies of love, in the streams that ran through groves of sacred myrtle.

Abstinence was demanded of the women in preparation for these sacred orgies. Wrote Aristophanes: "All the women who desired to take part in the festival were obliged to abstain from sexual intercourse for nine days before. The cleverness of the priests demanded this as an act of piety, the real reason of course being that the women, whipped up by their long abstinence, might be able to take part in erotic orgies with less restraint. To strengthen themselves in this chastity that was demanded of them, which they probably found hard enough to preserve, women laid cooling herbs and leaves in their bed, especially Agnus Castus and other plants. But according to Photius, at this time women ate garlic in order to frighten men away by the unappetizing smell of their mouth."

In Corinth the worship of the love goddess centered about the great temple of Aphrodite on the splendid summit of Acrocorinthus. The worship was conducted by priestesses of Aphrodite, courtesans who practiced their devotion in poverty, for all their earnings went into the coffers of their order. "As a result of this remarkable institution," writes Dr. Charles Seltman in *Women in Antiquity*,[33] "the girls of Corinthian Aphrodite were held in respect and honor among the Greeks as a whole. Some came from the class of free citizens, as Athenaeus pointed out, and others who had been purchased by donors were automatically freed by being given to the goddess herself. A measure of the respect in which they were held is the fact that an outstanding poet of the fifth century B.C., Pindar, wrote a eulogy for a number of Corinthian girls. It so happened that a rich Corinthian citizen, Xenophon, entered for two events at the Olympic Games in 464 B.C. after having promised his city goddess a present of twenty-five girls should he be successful. He won. He then asked Pindar to write him an ode. Yet it is amusing to reflect that Xenophon himself receives a bare mention at the very end, while Pindar put all his enthusiasm into writing a charming eulogy of "the gift" to the goddess.

> Young hospitable girls, beguiling creatures in wealthy Corinth,
> You who burn the amber tears of fresh frankincense
> Full often soaring upward in your souls to Aphrodite,
> Heavenly Mother of loves;
>
> To you girls she has granted
> Blamelessly upon lovely beds
> To cull the blossom of delicate bloom;
> For under love's necessity all things are fine.
>
> Yet I wonder whatever the lords of Corinth will be saying of me!
> Devising as I am a prelude to sweet song
> All for the pleasure of anybody's girls!
> But we've tested their gold with a pure touchstone.
>
> O Lady of Cyprus! Hither to your sanctuary
> Xenophon has brought fillies—
> A hundred limbs of girls—
> Glad for the fulfillment of his vows.

To these girls also a crabbed morality would doubtless apply the term "temple prostitute." Those who accept this terminology would do well to bear in mind the comment formulated by Gordon Rattray Taylor:

"The term prostitution with its connotation of sordid commercialism and hole-and-corner lusts wholly misrepresents the sacred and uplifted character of the experience as it was experienced by those who took part. It was nothing less than an act of communion with God (or godhead) and was as remote from sensuality as the Christian act of communion is remote from gluttony." [28]

At the festival of Aphrodite Anosia, celebrated in Thessaly, the males were excluded entirely and female homosexual acts were performed in honor of the goddess. This ceremony was characterized also by the use of erotic flagellation, a form of stimulation also used in the Roman rites of Bona Dea, as the frescoes in the House of the Mysteries at Pompeii attest. This purely feminine ritual may have begun as a staid and matronly worship of a fertility goddess, but, like so many rites in ancient Rome, it deteriorated into an orgy with overtones of perversity. These were the rites which aroused the indignation of Juvenal who described them with his characteristic venom:

"The rites of the Good Goddess! Shrieking flutes excite the women's loins, wine and the trumpet madden them, whirling and shrieking, rapt by Priapus. Then, then, their hearts are blazing with lust, their voices stammer with it, their wine gushes in torrents down their soaking thighs. . . . This is no mimicry, the thing is done in earnest: even Priam's aged loins and Nestor cold with age would burn to see it. Their itching cannot bear delay: This is sheer Woman, shrieking and crying everywhere in the hall, 'It is time, let in the men!' The lover sleeps . . . then let him snatch a greatcoat, hurry here. No? Then they rush upon the slaves. Not even slaves? Then a scavenger comes off the streets."

Love priestesses were not confined to the temples of Greece. To the east, beyond the plain of Mesopotamia, stood temples dedicated to Kama, the god of love, on which erotic symbols bloomed with a tropical luxuriance. At Khajuraho, on intricate spires of stones thick with intertwined figures, the endless manifestations of the primal force twist and turn among couples, copulations, full breasts, sinuous hips, erecting *lingams*, expanding *yonis*. Legs, arms, jewels, flowers, genitals riot in a complex blending of forms, a veritable orgy of creative energy (Fig. 25).

This orgy was not confined to the myriad stone figures carved on the outside of the temple. Within could be found the temple dancers, the Devadasi, servants of the Kama, whose only aim in life was to serve the deity in a sexual capacity. These girls were either courtesans bought by the temple trustees or girl children given to the temple by pious parents in keeping with some vow. The sun temples, famous for their erotic art, were no less famous for their dancing girls. The famous temple of Somnath had more than five hundred Devadasis. It was a pious act in India to dedicate beautiful girls to these temples, indeed the *Padmapurana* goes as far as to say that such a dedication is the surest way of winning the *suryaloka* (heaven of the sun god).

"However a girl came into the temple," wrote B. Z. Goldberg in *The Sacred Fire*, "she had a long period of training before her. This training was neither in religion nor in sex, but primarily in the graces of lovemaking and companionship. For the vocation of the temple priestess was complicated, indeed. She was catering not to the Western man, but to the man of the East whose loving was as refined as it was intricate.

"To the Occidental man, love is either highly spiritual— romance and chivalry—or purely physical, mere sexual union. The prostitute of the West answers the call of his physical love. She receives her guest in the dark and only for a brief moment. The man comes to her when his passions run high; the minute the passion is spent he leaves. The Chinese or Indian prostitute is first of all a companion and an entertainer. She will delight her guests intellectually by conversation, or artistically by playing or singing; she may dance and she may serve tea. What follows is a relationship gradually drifted into, not an act bought and paid for.

"The temple priestess is, therefore, trained for Oriental love-

25. Figures from the Kandarya Mahadeo Temple,
Khajuraho, India. "Legs, arms, jewels, flowers,
genitals riot in a complex blending of forms."

making. For ten hours each day the little girls are instructed in singing and dancing. From the age of seven or eight to fourteen or fifteen, they dance six times daily. They are taught, too, to acquire charm and poise and to make their bodies attractive through the use of fine clothes, sweet-scented powders, and delicate perfumes whose exotic fragrance enhance their allurement. Their minds are also trained and they become delightful conversationalists." [34]

A pen picture of the priestess in action is offered us by Savarin: "The suppleness of their bodies is inconceivable. One is astonished at the mobility of their features, to which they give at will an impression agreeable to the part they play. Their indecent attitudes are often carried to excess. Their looks, gestures, all speak in such an expressive manner that it is not possible to misunderstand what they mean. At the commencement of the dance they throw aside, with their veils, the modesty of their sex. A long, very light silken robe descends to their heels enclosed by a rich girdle. Their long black hair floats in perfumed tresses over their shoulders; a gauze chemise, almost transparent, veils their breasts. To the measure of their movements, the form and contours of their bodies are successively displayed. The sound of the flute, of the tambourine and cymbals, regulates their step and hastens or slows their motions. They are full of love and passion; they appear intoxicated; they are Bacchantes in delirium; then they seem to forget all restraint and give themselves up to the disorder of their senses."

SEX AND LIBERATION

The love priestesses of ancient Greece and the Devadasis of the Indian sun temples ministered to a deep yearning, the yearning for liberation, for inner freedom, which resides in the psyche of man and is, perhaps, one of his most distinguished characteristics. This urge is associated with the sex urge, but the association is neither direct nor simple. To understand it we must realize that the urge has, from the earliest times, manifested itself in two different ways, the way of discipline associated with Apollo and the way of ecstasy associated with Dionysus.

Between these two ways men have staggered like drunkards, reeling either too far in one direction or too far in the other. During the Apollonian phase man becomes an ascetic. He overcontrols his desires, "mortifies the flesh," refuses himself even normal indulgence in food or drink or sex. During the Dionysian phase he overindulged his desires, seeking liberation in an orgy of sex and drinking, worshipping the god Liber, the great liberator. He awakens exhausted, with a hangover, and for a time becomes an Apollonian. If he remains in the Apollonian phase for too long he becomes cold, rigid, censorious, the typical Puritan. If he remains in the Dionysian phase for too long he merely becomes debauched.

The most violent of the orgies in ancient Greece were celebrated by women. These orgies were the Dionysia, enacted in Cithaeron and Parnassus by women whom the Athenians called Bacchantes or Thyiads. "At night, attired in Bacchic costumes, goatskins, and with disheveled hair, and carrying musical instruments, they climbed to the summit of an adjoining mountain and, stimulated to abnormal activity and excitement by the wine which they otherwise seldom if ever drank, they performed on the heights dances and sacrifices which rapidly achieved the category of orgies." [35]

That these orgies were characterized by violence we are left in no doubt by several ancient authors. The god was worshipped as Dionysus Zagreus which means "torn to pieces." His violent end symbolized the apparent death of the vine when, shorn of its foliage by the winter storms, it becomes bare and seemingly barren. The rites, for this reason, represented the death of the god, and were wild to the point of savagery. The women who performed them, Bacchae, maenads, Thyiads, wandered through woods and mountains, their flying locks crowned with ivy, brandishing wands and torches, to the hollow sound of the drum and shrill notes of the flute, with wild dances, insane cries and jubilation. Victims of the sacrifice, oxen, goats, even fauns and roes which were captured in the forest, were killed, torn to pieces, and eaten raw.

We may guess that in earlier, more savage times, this treatment was meted out not only to goats and fauns but to youths who played the role of Dionysus in the orgies. Such is the interpretation of the Theseus myth by Mary Renault in *The King Must Die*.[36] The myth states that Theseus abandoned Ariadne on the island of Naxos where she was married to Dionysus. Actually the island was the center of a Dionysus cult and Ariadne's "marriage" may well have terminated in the tearing to pieces of the youth who played the role of Dionysus, and the devouring of his flesh. Theseus, in this novel, thus describes Ariadne, after the orgy:

"I could not see her mouth, for the blood all over it; I saw her teeth, even, crusted with dried blood. As I bent over her, its stale reek met me mixed with the smell of wine . . . She stretched out her hand. It lay closed on her breast, like a child's who has taken her toy to bed with her. Now when she tried to spread it out, the blood on it had stuck between the fingers, and she could not part them. But she opened her palm and then I saw what she was holding."

The object, which made the redoubtable Theseus vomit his heart out and leave Naxos and Ariadne for ever, was presumably a human phallus torn from the body of the youth who had played the role of the god. That such savagery could be accepted by the ancient Greeks as god-inspired should not seem too strange to members of a contemporary cult addicted to drinking a god's blood, eating his flesh and making a solemn mystery out of the process. But the sacramental bread and wine of the Christians are a far cry from the cannibalism of the Dionysian orgies. The latter involved "passing beyond oneself," a condition of ecstasy, and in that state, it appears, anything was permitted.

"The Greek, when he was seized by some force compelling him to act in a manner different from that which he would normally have chosen, explained his sensations, naturally enough, as 'possession by the gods.'

"Unlike the Romans, this feeling inspired the Greeks with feelings of admiration rather than of obedience, but it did cause them to value everything which led to the achievement of a state of 'theolepsy'; of communions with the deity. This explains what to modern minds is at first difficult to comprehend, how the Greeks could regard indulgence in alcohol, dancing and copulation with sentiments of religious awe." [35]

The destructive cult of Dionysus Zagreus had its Oriental counterpart in the cult of Kali in India. Kali, the black goddess, is not only the universal mother but also the destroyer of all her children. Wreathed in skulls and chains of severed heads she dances on the corpse of her husband flourishing a dagger. The worshippers of this, her destructive aspect, called themselves Thugs and contributed to the limitation of the population by ceremoniously strangling any traveler who happened to offer them an opportunity to practice this art. By the time the British in India put a stop to the practice the Thugs had destroyed a sizable number of their compatriots. It seems reasonable to assume that the motivating force behind these ritual murders was a distorted form of sex energy, similar to that which drove the Bacchae and maenads to their bloody excesses on the islands of Greece.

SEX ENERGY TRANSMUTED

Crude worship of the sex force, exemplified by orgiastic rites or worship of the *lingam* or the *yoni*, is only one aspect of the deification of sex energy. More subtle forms of this deification can be found in Tibet, or in the temples of Sikkim or Nepal. Here the mystic Tantric teaching has mingled with the calmer doctrines of Mahayana Buddhism, and expressed itself in sexual symbols of astonishing complexity. The primal energy, manifesting in its tranquil or dynamic aspects, *shiva* and *shakti* united in the four positions of *maithuna* which only the gods can assume without strain, are depicted amid a wealth of allegory intelligible only to the initiate. Here, in a fury of energy, the Padma Heruka, reddish-brown in color, furious in aspect, leaping on one foot, in full sexual union with a *shakti* as terrible as himself, tramples underfoot two corpses on a lotus and solar throne surrounded by flames of wisdom. Maha Kala, the Lord of Time, thousand-armed and many-faced, creator and destroyer in one, cavorts on one leg in the fury of the cosmic dance, whirling amid arcs of flame, clutching a white *shakti* with one of his numerous arms. *Matam Rudra*, whose second aspect is Yama, Judge of the Dead, black or deep blue in color, ferocious in aspect, flourishes with his right hand the sacred sword, clutches in his left a skull cap filled to the brim with blood, glares through all three eyes at the illusory world of *maya*, a chain of severed heads about his neck, a crown of skulls on his head, on his lips the symbolic sneer and in his embrace, coupled in sexual union, a dark blue *shakti*, three-eyed and terrifying as himself, leaping on the crimson disk of the lotus throne totally surrounded by flames. Here at the apex of the sacred mandala, in a woolly white cloud-land floating against a tranquil sky, the One, the Uncreated, the Existing-for-Himself, Adi-Buddha, who is Vajradhara, who is Dorje-chang, sits on the solar disk of the lotus throne, dark blue in color, in his right hand the *dorje*, in his left the bell, embracing his *shakti*, white in color and naked who is Prajna Paramita, the perfect Gnosis whose nakedness symbolizes detachment from bondage to form, whose femaleness is to his maleness what the bell is to the *dorje*, what wisdom is to method, what practice is to knowledge.

Here the great schism is healed. The nature of man, first divided by Sumerian dualism and further fragmented by the Judeo-Christian Guilt Cult, attains, in the unions of those symbolic forms, the poise, wholeness and essential beauty absent from the majority of human unions. The balanced couplings of these Eastern deities are the outward and visible manifestation of an inward power existing in man quite unsuspected except by a few adepts, most of them cloistered in remote places far from the crowd. The sexual force, so runs this ancient teaching, is a manifestation of another profounder power. Average sensual man knows nothing about it, is the slave of the subtle power and, used by that power, is compelled to pour out his life juice in hairy couplings to which Lawrence Durrell applied the words "tragic and ludicrous." As a great magician, holding his audience spellbound, can cause them to see things not really there, so this force that lies, as it were, behind sex energy, throws on the screen of the mind a succession of forms, some loathsome, some desirable, all taken for real by the hypnotized observer. He is the prince of dreams, this hidden magician, night dreams, daydreams, dry dreams, wet dreams. The hypnotized victim of his power lives enmeshed in these dreams, enchanted by the forms the magician creates.

Not so the adept.

To such a one the bubbling ferment in the loins is a challenge, a summons to perform the supreme creative act. The servile obsession with sin that characterizes the devotee of the Judeo-Christian Guilt Cult has no place in the spirit of the adept. The whole idea of sin, impurity, unchastity, uncleanness has for him no relevance whatsoever. It is merely another product of the working of that great magician in the psyche who uses his magical powers to make that seem foul which more usually seems fair.

The learned sexologist may criticize such concepts and express the opinion that such myths are strictly for mystics who prefer to delude themselves with colorful fairy tales rather than assimilate harsh unromantic facts. To these the adept would reply that one dare not, if one claims to be an unprejudiced investigator, lightly dismiss the products of five millennia of Indian culture, for this knowledge seems to reach all the way back to Harrappa, the lost civilization of the Indus Valley, in which the art and science of yoga seem first to have been discovered.

What then is this secret power of which the copulatory activities of all mankind are merely a by-product? The master science that deals with the transmuting of sexual energy, depicts in the body of man a chain of psychic centers (*chakras*) (Fig. 26). A decorative convention portrays these centers as lotuses each having a different color, a different number of petals. Actually there are no colors, no sounds. These are merely allegories. The psychic centers are storage batteries for

26. *The chain of seven* chakras *or psychic centers.*

different energy substances and have both an endocrine (glandular) and a nervous (neuronal) aspect.

In Indian literature all this is described in highly figurative language, often embellished with so many fantastic claims that the sober Western student feels revulsion. Offensive or not, such is the *mode* of this literature. It tends to be rapturous. The words should not be taken over-seriously. The works here to be quoted were never intended to be more than summaries to be filled out and elaborated upon by the teacher in accordance with the type, ability and degree of progress of the student. This study was never intended to be merely intellectual. The truth or otherwise of these statements was something the student had to prove for himself by effort, practice and observation.

What then is this ultimate energy of which the sexual act is but one manifestation? Here is a colorful account (highly allegorical) drawn from a masterwork on yoga (*Hatha Yoga Pradipika*).[37]

"As a door is opened with a key, so the Yogi opens the door to liberation by awakening Kundalini by Hatha Yoga. Kundalini sleeps, covering with her mouth the hole of the passage by which one can go to the seat of Brahma which is free from pains. Kundalini Sakti sleeps on the bulb for the purpose of giving liberation to yogis and bondage to the ignorant . . . the bulb is above the anus, three inches in extent and appears as if a folded cloth. This sleeping she-serpent should be awakened by catching hold of her tail. By the force of Hatha the Sakti leaves her sleep and starts upwards. This she-serpent is situated in the Muladhara."

To this may be added an additional quote from the *Gheranda Samhita*: [38]

"The great goddess Kundalini, the energy of the Self (*atman*), sleeps in the Muladhara; she has the form of a serpent having three coils and a half. So long as she is asleep in the body the *jiva* (individual self) is a mere animal and true knowledge does not arise . . . As by a key a door is opened, so by awakening the Kundalini by Hatha Yoga the door of Brahma is unlocked."

The full flavor of this strange Oriental teaching is given by this passage from the *Siva Samhita*.[39]

"With strong inspiration fix the mind on the *Muladhara chakra*. Then engage in contracting the *yoni*, which is situated in the perineal space. Then let him contemplate the God of Love, as situated in the Brahma *yoni*, beautiful as the Banduk flower, brilliant as tens of millions of suns and cool as tens of millions of moons. Above the *yoni* is a very small and subtle flame, whose form is intelligence. Let him imagine that a union takes place between himself and that flame (the Siva and Sakti). Then imagine that there passes through the central *nada* (Susumna) the three bodies in their due order (etheric, astral, mental). In every *chakra* nectar is emitted the characteristic of which is great bliss. Its color is whitish-rose, full of splendor, showering down in jets of immortal fluid. Let him drink this wine of immortality which is divine then again enter the perineal space through the practice of *pranayama* . . .

"Those who wish for emancipation should practice this daily. Through practice (*abhyasa*), success is obtained, through practice one gains liberation. Perfect consciousness is gained through practice. Yoga is attained through practice; success in *mudras* comes by practice; through practice is gained success in *pranayama*. Death can be cheated of its prey through practice and man becomes the conqueror of death by practice. Through practice one gets the power of prophecy, and the power of going everywhere, through mere exertion of will. This *Yoni Mudra* should be kept in great secrecy, and not be given to everybody. Even when threatened with death, it should not be revealed or given to others."

Closely allied to this practice (awakening of Kundalini) is the art of sexual yoga, derived from the highly ritualized forms of sexual union which have been practiced in India since Vedic times. "I am the heaven, thou the earth," says the husband to the wife (*Brhadaranyaka Upanishad*). Viewed in this way the sexual union became a sacred ceremony, involving preliminary purifications and prayers. The woman was transfigured and became the consecrated place where the sacrifice is performed: "Her lap is a sacrificial altar; her hairs the sacrificial grass; her skin the soma press. The two lips of the vulva are the fire. As great as is the world of him who sacrifices with the Vajapeya sacrifice, so great the world of him who practices sexual intercourse, knowing this."

It was this attitude toward sex that led to the development of sexual yoga. Yoga means union. The word is derived from the same root as the word yoke, as used in the term "yoke of oxen." The union referred to is that ultimate blending in which the separate self merges with the universal self. This is *samadhi*, or, in Buddhist terminology, entry into *nirvana*. That such an ultimate blending might be attainable through the disciplined use of sex energy should surprise no one who is at all familiar with the utterances of the mystics. Even Christian mystics, though warped in their attitude toward sex by their excessive preoccupation with guilt and sin, tend to use erotic language to describe some of their experiences.

"Every naked woman incarnates *prakriti*. Hence she is to be looked upon with the same adoration and the same detachment that one exercises in pondering the unfathomable secret of nature, its limitless capacity to create. The ritual nudity of the *yogini* has an intrinsic mystical value: if, in the presence of the naked woman, one does not find in one's inmost being the same terrifying emotion that one feels before the revelation of the cosmic mystery, there is no rite, there is only a secular act, with all the familiar consequences (strengthening of the karmic chain, etc.)." [40]

Such, in the words of Mircea Eliade, is the attitude which underlies the practice of sexual yoga. The *yogini* (female yogi) has been specially instructed in the role she must play. She assumes, from the standpoint of her partner as well as her own, the role of the Divine Woman, the universal passive principal, the second part of the dyad, *purusha-prakriti* or energy-matter. She becomes *shakti* itself, that subtle power the correct use of which leads to liberation. She is, in alchemical terms, the second part of the *androgyne*, the completed being, the unified, the One. In uniting with her the yogi experiences the unity and enjoys the supreme bliss (*maha sukha*).

Such an experience, however, is not attained easily. *Maithuna*, devotional love, must never end in seminal emission or the yogi loses all the energy generated by his practice. The neophyte prepares for this experience by mastering the three controls, control of thought, control of breath, control of semen. In his mind he transforms the girl into a goddess through a process which Eliade calls "an interiorized iconographic dramaturgy." In this way sexual union is transformed into a ritual through which the human couple becomes a divine couple. "Prepared for the performance of the rite (*maithuna*) by the meditation and the ceremonies that make it possible and fruitful, he (i.e., the yogin) considers the yogini, his companion and mistress, under the name of some Bhagavati, as the substitute and the very essence of Tara, sole source of joy and rest. The mistress synthesizes the entire nature of woman, she is mother, sister, wife, daughter; in her voice, demanding love, the officiant recognizes the voices of the Bhagavatis supplicating Vajrasattva. Such, for both the Saiva and Buddha Tantric schools, is the way of salvation, of *bodhi*. The *mudra*, wife of the yogin, chosen according to established rules, offered and consecrated by the *guru*, must be young, beautiful and learned: with her, the disciple will perform the ceremony, scrupulously observing the *siksas*, for if no salvation is possible without love, bodily union does not suffice to bring salvation."

Maithuna, which is simply the Sanskrit word for sexual union, is, in this form, a complex ritual depending for its effect on a mastery of the practice known in the West as *coitus reservatus.* As such it was described by Aldous Huxley in his novel *Island,*[41] in which this particular practice was used to make possible unlimited sexual love without a population explosion. The technique was also employed by members of the original Oneida community who practiced a form of sexual communism. Physiologically speaking, *coitus reservatus* and the closely related art of *carezza* involve a control of the nervous mechanisms which normally build up sexual tension and result in the male orgasm. The orgasmic energy is stored up and can be used in other ways. However, only an adept in yoga knows how to make use of the force thus accumulated. For those not having the necessary knowledge it is doubtful whether the practice is of any value.

A curious development of sexual yoga is the practice of *vajroli,* which may be roughly translated as "return of the semen," an exercise of importance in "left-hand" Tantrism. The practice involves gaining control over the urinary bladder in such a way that it becomes possible to dilate it at will. One who has mastered *vajroli* can draw back into his body the semen he has just expended. The practice is employed in Tibet as well as India and is described as follows by Alexandra David-Neel:

"A certain class of Tibetan occultists teach a mode of training that is half physical and half psychic, comprising such strange practices as causing the return into the body of the seminal fluid, or reabsorbing it when it has actually been ejected.

"Curious reasons are alleged in explanation of the utility of these exercises. In the first case, it is not simply a matter of retaining within oneself the energy which Tibetans regard as being contained in the seed of life—for ascetics who strictly practice celibacy do this naturally—but of exciting this latent energy and then refraining from expending it. In the second case, it is said that the energy inherent in the sperm may be enriched, during coition, with an element of feminine energy which it appropriates to itself and carries away with it when reabsorption takes place.

"Some imagine that in this way they can practice a kind of subtle vampirism by engrossing the psychic force of those women marked with special signs, whom they look upon as incarnate fairies." [42]

The curious practice resulted, we may guess, from the excessive regard paid to the *bindu* or seed by primitive people who regarded it as synonymous with the life force. "The yogi who can protect his *bindu* thus overcomes death; because death comes by discharging *bindu,* and life is prolonged by its preservation" (*Hatha Yoga Pradipika*). There is not a shadow of scientific evidence to support this opinion. Semen is produced by the male body like saliva, gastric juice or any other secretion, and whether it is stored or expended does not appear to affect the length of life. *Vajroli* is certainly a curious example of the sort of physiological control that a determined practitioner can attain, but it remains merely a trick and one, moreover, which can lead to infection of the bladder by the introduction of microorganisms from the vagina.

TANTRIC ORGIES

The decorous union of yogi and yogini, carefully prepared for in advance, is not the only manifestation of sex energy in Indian mystical practice. The "abandoned woman," the courtesan, the washerwoman (*dombi*), also figures. The more depraved and debauched the woman, the more fit she is for the rite. *Dombi,* "the washerwoman," is a favorite of the Tantric writers. "O *dombi,* thou art all besoiled . . . Some call thee ugly . . . But the wise clasp thee to their bosoms . . . O *dombi*! no woman is more dissolute than thou!" This predilection for courtesans and washerwomen is explained by the Tantric doctrine of the identity of opposites. The "noblest and most precious" is hidden in the "basest and most common."

The Tantras are a group of Hindu scriptures written specifically for man in the *kalijuga*. *Kalijuga*, the last of the four ages, is an age of evil. "Men of this age are marked by their depraved tendencies. They love what is evil, and detest what is good; religious duty is neglected, and men develop an insatiable thirst for sensuous pleasures. Kings persecute their subjects, and the subjects rise in rebellion against the rulers. Nations wage war on nations and all perish through violence. Brahmins forsake the study of Vedas for the pursuit of pleasures and wealth, and low-born men usurp the thrones of virtuous monarchs of noble blood. Friendship degenerates into mutual exploitation; and desire becomes the only attachment between men and women.

The Tantrics maintain that there is a certain amount of fatality in this state of affairs. Men have fallen so low that they are rendered incapable of realizing their fall. Hence the Tantrics tell us that the high precepts of the Vedic times are inapplicable to the men of *kalijuga* who are so stupid that they can neither understand nor appreciate them. According to them, the Vedic rites were meant for the *kritajuga*, the Smritis (like the codes of Manu, Parasara, etc.) for the *thretajuga*, and the Puranas for the *dwaparajuga*. For the *kalijuga*, we are told, the most important, in fact the only texts that can be followed with profit are the Tantras. Pleasure and religious merit seldom go together. The Tantras, however, ensure both:

"Where there is worldly enjoyment there is no liberation; where there is liberation there is no worldly enjoyment. But in the case of the excellent devotees of Sri Sundari (a form of Shakti) both liberation and enjoyment are in the hollow of their hands." [43]

It was to make religion attractive to the spiritually deformed man of the *kalijuga* that the ritual of the Tantric circle (Chakrapuja or Circle Worship) was offered. The ritual, says the author of the *Kama Kalpa,* is usually performed at night in the house of a wealthy devotee. A room is cleaned and consecrated for the worship and a circle of a certain radius is drawn on the floor. Within the circle is inscribed a mystic diagram (*yantra*). Within the diagram sits the host and his *shakti,* the *shakti* (female) being seated on the left of the *shakta* (male). The *shakti* may be either the man's wife or some other woman, for every woman is a living embodiment of *shakti.*

The ritual is based on the five M's which are *madya* or wine, *mansa* or meat, *matsya* or fish, *mudra* or corn and *maithuna* or sexual intercourse. First the *kalasha* or wine jar is brought in and, after being filled and consecrated, is placed in front of the host and his *shakti* on a jeweled altar enclosed in a mystic diagram. After the consecration of the wine the cooked meat, fish and corn are brought in in large quantities and blessed by incantations and appropriate mystic gestures (*mudras*). Drinking begins. The devotee eats meat with the first cup, fish with the second, corn with the third, all these with the fourth and whatever he desires with the fifth.

The *Mahanirvana Tantra* calls a halt to the drinking at this point, declaring that five cups of wine are enough for anyone. "They may not drink until the sight or the mind is affected. To drink to excess is bestial." But the *Mahanirvana Tantra* is one of the mildest of these scriptures and there can be little doubt that the rite frequently takes the form of a Dionysian orgy, indeed one of the purposes of the rite is to raise the devotee to a state that is beyond good and evil. After the first four M's have been adequately indulged in, the final M— *maithuna*—takes place beteween each male and his *shakti.*

The members of the Tantric circle (at least among practitioners of the left-hand cult, *vama margis*) insist on complete secrecy in worship. Nevertheless rumors about what went on during the Tantric orgies spread among the former rulers of India and shocked the worthy British to the depths of their proper Anglican souls. Tantra, for this reason, acquired a vaguely sinister connotation, as did the bacchanalian rites in ancient Rome. Their sinister quality was further exaggerated by the almost complete ignorance of the critics about what really took place.

This ignorance was partly dispelled by the labors of Sir John Woodruff who, writing under the name of Arthur Avalon, made the texts available in English translation and illuminated the Tantric practices with his commentaries. He compared the "shameless indulgence" in meat, wine and sexual intercourse to the homeopathic idea of destroying poison by means of poison. A more modern analogy would be that of using the attenuated organisms of disease (virus or bacteria) to generate an immunity against that disease.

"Man under the influence of wine becomes devoid of manliness and worthless. The stupefying power of wine and woman is so great as to attract even the pious and wise and hurl them into the abyss of darkness and ignorance. Here Shiva (the propounder of the Tantric system) prescribes poison which eradicates poison. We know as other Sadhakas do that this homeopathic system of Shiva is infallible and yields speedy results. He who thirsts for wine or lusts after women can be cured by this treatment within a very short time. But the physician, that is the Guru, must be experienced and skillful. A slight error in the administration of the poison may lead to fatal result. On this account Shiva said that the path of Kaula rite is more difficult than it is to walk on the edge of a sword or to embrace the neck of a tiger."

The Kaula rite, as this Tantric practice is called (*Kaula* in Sanskrit means either ancient or noble), is, like the Magic Theater in Hesse's *Steppenwolf*, definitely *not for everybody*. No one who is not a *tatvajnani* (Knower of Secret Truths) can master the inner meaning of the rite. Those who practice it without the necessary preparation and inner knowledge merely become drunkards and libertines. No one would dare claim that the organisms of disease are not harmful. But if they are prepared in the right way (as in a vaccine) they become instrumental in protecting the body against disease. So the

Tantric rite and sexual yoga in general trains the participant to use one of the most powerful physiological forces (sex energy) not for the propagation of a race which is already far too numerous, but for the attainment of a higher state of consciousness in which the petty personal ego is transcended.

**IV.
SEX ENERGY
DEGRADED**

ANTI-EROS AND THE DEATH WISH

MAN IS, I suppose, the only living creature which has found reasons for deliberately inhibiting his sexual drive. The bull does not hesitate to mount the cow, nor sit moping in the corner of the field. The flower does not primly close its petals against the pollen-bearing bee. That man should hedge the sexual drive with rules designed to protect the rights, or fancied rights, of individuals is natural; but that he should claim a special virtue in complete abstinence from sexual activity is a paradox which calls for close examination." [28]

It does indeed. The above quotation from Rattray Taylor's *Sex in History* focuses attention on what might be called man's supreme biological absurdity. Such an absurdity can be perpetrated only by the human. He alone among the living things of earth has power by virtue of his presumptuous and meddlesome roof brain to interfere with instinctive mechanisms that evolved long before the cerebral cortex became predominant. In no area has this interference been more disastrous than that of sex. There are, it is true, destructive manifestations of sex energy at levels below the human. The female mantis devouring her mate is perhaps the most extreme example of this destructiveness. But only man has built from the negative elements in his own psyche a system of maleficent delusions centering around the sexual function. The same human mind which, in some cultures, deified sex energy and revered the sex organs as manifestations of the divine in other cultures degraded this energy and turned it into a source of madness and death.

To an impartial biologist few areas of human behavior are more distasteful to study than that which can loosely be called the anti-sex or anti-Eros. What makes the subject so unpleasant is that this force in human society makes no sense at all. It is unbiological, unphysiological, unethical and unreasonable. It violates every natural law, is ugly, depressing, disgusting, pointless, fruitless.

So the biologist can hardly be blamed if he wishes he could omit from his studies an account of anti-sex, the manifestations of which are so unbiological. However, he has no choice if he wants to be honest. A work on sex energy must deal with all the aspects of sex energy, even when, by a ludicrous and pathological twist, this life-giving energy is turned back to front and converted into an instrument of death.

Moreover the forces of the anti-sex are still very active in our society. They do not (thank Venus) manifest today in the hideous forms they took in the seventeenth century. It would be unthinkable for us to condemn a girl of sixteen to have her breasts burned off in public and then to be totally consumed in a larger fire for having had sexual intercourse with a demon (a sentence imposed by a German judge, a pious Christian, in 1639 A.D.). No. We are civilized people. We no longer burn individuals. Entire cities, yes. But not young girls in public for coupling with demons.

We are even allowed, by the special dispensation of our learned jurists, to read books in which the sexual act is described, provided the account is not calculated to arouse "lewd and lascivious imaginings." This is progress indeed and might lull the unwary reader into thinking that the great, mad forces of anti-sex have been dispersed, that those industrious dung beetles, rolling their gathered pellets of shame and guilt, have finally retreated into their holes and will plague us no longer.

Perhaps this really has happened in some countries, but

certainly it has not happened in these United States. Here the voice of the devotees of the anti-sex is still loud and strident. Every step that is taken toward a sounder attitude to sex evokes from these old crows a chorus of squawks and croaks. And because the aforesaid crows are often influential in society their croaks may have far-reaching effects. They are a power, no doubt about it.

This being so, it becomes more than ever necessary to examine the manifestations of anti-sex in all their hideousness: one must know one's enemy in order to defeat him. What, then, is the origin of this peculiar force in man which causes him to deny himself one of the supreme physical satisfactions, and to brand this satisfaction evil and impure? Rattray Taylor, in the above-mentioned study, makes much of the Freudian dyad, Eros and Thanatos. Eros is the creative force, manifesting both as love and as lust. Thanatos is the destructive force, the death wish, the great negation.

So what is the anti-sex which includes fear of sex in all its manifestations, disgust with sex, renunciation of sex? Can we regard it as an aspect of the death wish directed not against the individual but against the race as a whole? Does the "keeper of conscience," the vengeful, prohibiting superego that binds with its chains the exuberant id, supply the force from which the anti-sex draws its strength?

This interpretation may be correct, but it leaves several questions unanswered. The ancient Greeks, at the festival of Dionysus, or the Romans at the festival of Father Liber, carried the great phallus with religious awe and made obeisance to the object as a symbol of divine force. Were the members of these ancient civilizations free of the manifestations of the death wish? Did the superego, with its long string of "thou-shalt-nots" play no part in the operation of their pagan psyches?

We can hardly make such an assumption. If the death wish is a real element in the human psyche and not an artificial concept dreamed up by Freud then we must surely admit that both these ancient cultures were loaded with it. The Greeks, with their insane aggressiveness and absurd local patriotism, hurled themselves at one another's throats as if bent on committing communal suicide. The Romans so reveled in death that they made its public affliction one of their main sources of entertainment. And we can hardly assume that the people of these cultures were devoid of the superego, if this shadowy entity really exists. There were plenty of prohibitions in the ancient world and the superego was presumably necessary to ensure that these prohibitions were not totally disregarded.

The cultures of Polynesia at the time they were discovered by the white man were so devoid of sexual shame and guilt that the public performance of the sex act was a proper part of their religious celebrations. Were these communities untainted by the death wish? Far from it. Their inter-island wars were even more insanely destructive than those of the Greeks and the sacrifices they performed would have shamed Agamemnon. The superego manifested through a host of taboos that made life almost unbelievably complicated. Even so they did not suffer from sexual guilt and all the efforts of the ministers of the Judeo-Christian Guilt Cult have not been successful in infecting their psyches with this disease.

So it seems an oversimplification to state that the anti-sex in man is nothing more than an expression of the Freudian death wish. It is an aberration of the psyche which has developed in some cultures but not in others. To understand it we must study its historical origins.

THE CULT OF CYBELE

Did the anti-Eros manifest itself in antiquity before Christianity with its accompanying Guilt Cult became a dominant religion in the Western world? Of the ancient cultures we can say little. There is no sign of sex guilt in Homer. Herodotus, a very sex-conscious historian, makes no mention of the phenomenon. Should we attribute to the anti-Eros the excesses of the priests of Cybele? Consider the following account from *The Golden Ass* of Apuleius:

"They would throw their heads forward so that their long hair fell down over their faces, then rotate so rapidly that it wheeled round in a circle. Every now and then they would bite themselves savagely and as a climax cut their arms with the sharp knives that they carried. One of them let himself go more ecstatically than the rest. Heaving deep sighs from the very bottom of his lungs, as if filled with the spirit of the goddess, he pretended to go stark mad. (A strange notion, this, that divine immanency, instead of doing men good, enfeebles and disorders their senses; but if you will read on you will see how Providence eventually intervened to punish these charlatans.) He began by making a bogus confession of guilt, crying out in prophetic tones that he had in some way offended against the holy laws of his religion. Then he called on his own hands to inflict the necessary punishment and snatching up one of the whips that these half-men always carry, the sort with several long strands of woolen yarn strung with sheep's knuckle bones, gave himself a terrific flogging. The ground was slippery with the blood that oozed from the knife-cuts and the wounds made by the flying bones, but he bore the pain with amazing fortitude." [44]

The passage is certainly suggestive and might lead one to conclude that the worship of Cybele, the "Syrian Goddess," was a sort of Guilt Cult deriving its emotional force from anti-sex. The fury of the attack on the self indicates that very powerful psychic energies were involved, perhaps the same Dionysian frenzy that underlay the great orgies performed in honor of this god. That the Dionysian frenzy could be destructive as well as creative was shown during the rites of Zagreus, when fawns or kids were torn to pieces by the maddened maenads. This same fury was directed against themselves by the priests of Cybele and took the form of a specifically sexual attack. For these castrate priests were not emasculated by their fellows. They slashed off their sexual organs with their own hands. We have Lucian's word for it.

"As the priests sing and celebrate their orgies, frenzy falls on some of them, and many who had come as mere spectators afterwards are found to have committed the great act. I shall narrate what they do. Any young man who has resolved on this action strips off his clothes and with a loud shout bursts into the midst of the crowd and picks up a sword from a number of swords which I suppose have been kept for many years for this purpose. He takes it and castrates himself and runs wild through the city bearing in his hands what he has cut off. He casts it into any house at will and from this house receives woman's raiment and ornaments."

What savagery! What frenzy! The lukewarm modern, whose strongest religious raptures are limited to a once-a-week hymn and psalm routine and a mild fast in Lent, must stand amazed before such passion. To cut off one's genitals—penis, scrotum, testicles and all—and then run howling and bleeding through the town to deposit the relic in some neighbor's front yard, what motivation underlies such an act? What could it have been but sex-guilt, the anti-Eros? The whole thing started with the story of Attis who promised Cybele to remain always a boy (sexually immature). He was enticed into lustful intercourse by a local naiad, then, in a frenzy of self-reproach, cut out his manhood. Ovid described the event in verse.

> And now with a sharp stone he cut his body,
> Dragging his long hair in the filthy dust,
> And crying: "I deserve to bleed and suffer!
> Perish the member that made me forsworn!
> Away with it!" he cut away his manhood
> Leaving no sign to show he once was male.
> His madness still is copied, and his servants
> Cut their vile bodies while they toss their hair.

This outburst by young Attis lacks some of the anti-sexual vigor of the later utterances of the Christian Fathers. The young man was disturbed rather by his failure to keep the oath than by a specific loathing for all things sexual. But the savagery of his attacks on his own sex organs shows that the anti-Eros was already at work. And the cult of Cybele, with its frenzies of flagellation and self-mutilation can logically be regarded as a pagan guilt cult, analogous in many respects to the far more potent and widespread Guilt Cult that grew like a monstrous tumor on the body of Christianity.

CLEAN AND UNCLEAN

The historical development of the Guilt Cult has been described in detail by Gordon Rattray Taylor in *Sex in History* and one can hardly do better than follow his account. It is clear that the religion of the Jews, afflicted with a jealous father-god and bristling with prohibitions, provided conditions suitable for the development of a Guilt Cult. Of all the people of antiquity the Jews were most prone to feelings of guilt. That guilt, however, did not attach itself to sexual doings until a series of shattering disasters darkened the world-view of the Chosen People, causing them to despair of ever attaining happiness in the present world.

The earlier, more cheerful attitude of the Jews was exemplified by the advice offered by the writer of the Book of Ecclesiastes: "Go thy way, eat thy bread, and drink thy wine with a merry heart; for God hath already accepted thy works . . . Live joyfully with the wife whom thy lovest all the days of the life of thy vanity; for that is thy portion in life . . . Whatsoever thy hand findeth to do, do it with thy might, for there is no work, no device, nor knowledge, nor wisdom, in thy grave, wither thou goest."

This cheerful hedonism was linked, as the above passage so clearly shows, with a confident assumption that this earthly life is all man has and he had better get the most he can out of it. But the exile in Babylon seems to have wrought a change in the Jewish outlook. A tendency developed to view this earthly life as a sorry thing at best. It was foolish to expect much from such a condition, better in every way to await the resurrection and the coming of the Kingdom of the Messiah in which the lion would lie down with the lamb and a little child would lead them. And because it was good to live in hope of the Kingdom it became wrong to take delight in earthly pleasures. Gradually there developed the view that any pleasure was sinful, especially sexual pleasure. Reuben speaks of "the power of procreation and sexual intercourse with which, through love of pleasure, sin enters in . . ." Though previously rabbinical tradition had regarded celibacy as a crime we now find utterances praising virginity—"Happy is the barren that is undefiled . . . and happy is the eunuch." This tendency found its extreme expression in the behavior of that sect concerning which Josephus wrote as follows:

"These Essenes reject pleasure as evil, but esteem continence and the conquest over our passions to be virtue. They neglect wedlock but choose out other persons' children, while they are pliable, and fit for learning . . . They do not absolutely deny the fitness of marriage, and the succession of mankind thereby continued; but they guard against the lascivious behavior of women, and are persuaded that none of them preserve their fidelity to one man." [45]

A Guilt Cult had arisen and it grew apace. Life became cluttered with more and more religious minutiae. The idea of purity became an obsession and regulations relating to "uncleanness" multiplied. Suspicion relating to sexual matters became progressively more widespread. Boys should not even be allowed to play with girls. A mother-in-law should not live with her married daughter in case she seduced the latter's husband. Exposure of the privates was regarded as a crime and total nudity was thought even more obscene and shameful. Masturbation was defined in the Zohar as the worst sin of all, declared by one authority to be a crime meriting death. A Jew was advised not to sleep on his back, not to wear tight trousers and not to touch his penis while urinating for fear of provoking an involuntary discharge.

THE CURSE OF ROME

Jewish preoccupation with impurity was one of the elements that later contributed to the growth of anti-sex in Christendom. Another element was contributed by ancient Rome. It was in Rome, especially Rome of the first century A.D., that the normal sex impulse became most heavily contaminated with negative, destructive elements. An appalling taste for the affliction of pain took possession of the Roman psyche at the very time when Roman power had become dominant in the world. There was nothing the Roman of this period enjoyed better than watching a butchery of man by man in the arena. "Cold steel for the crowd, no quarter, and the amphitheater will end up looking like a slaughterhouse," as one of the characters in the *Satyricon* put it, adding that, as a special treat they would see Glyco's steward torn to pieces by the beasts.

A series of more or less mad rulers, Tiberius, Caligula, Nero, Domitian, set examples that the race as a whole was happy to follow. "As a sample of his humor," wrote Suetonius of Caligula, "he took his place beside a statue of Jupiter, and asked the tragic actor Apelles which of the two seemed to him the greater, and when he hesitated, Caligula had him flayed with whips, extolling his voice from time to time, when the wretch begged for mercy, as passing sweet even in his groans. Whenever he kissed the neck of his wife or sweetheart, he would say: "Off comes this beautiful head whenever I give the word." He even used to threaten now and then that he would resort to torture if necessary, to find out from his dear Caesonia why he loved her so passionately."

Cruelty combined with sexual perversion was even more apparent in the life of Nero. The emperor had the youth Sporus castrated and married him, then was himself married (in the role of the bride) to his freedman, "going so far as to imitate the cries and lamentations of a maiden being deflowered. . . . He also devised a kind of game, in which, covered with the skin of some wild animal, he was let loose from a cage and attacked private parts of men and women who were bound to stakes." (Suetonius)

With such examples before them it was hardly surprising that sexual cruelty was rampant among the Romans. Burgo Partridge in his *History of Orgies* draws attention to this sickness in the Roman psyche, a sickness to which the whole culture ultimately succumbed.

"According to Rosenbaum, large numbers of prostitutes used to assemble in brothels near the Circus Maximus for the purpose of intercepting men who were returning from the games, men who had been raised to a high pitch of sexual excitement by the gladiatorial shows, the mutilations by and of wild animals, and all the other obsessional insanities of the arena. One of the most prominent, repellent and characteristic features of these ceremonies was the organization, the high degree of ritual with which they were performed. It is this, the elaboration, the planning, the constant devising of new implements of torture, the odious ceremony, which brands the Romans as perverts. Into every newly invented mode of execution, into every torture was always brought one feature, the flogging of the victim or of the condemned man. It was not enough to be killed. Death was nothing, a mere negation. There must be positive pain first. 'Strike so that he feels he is dying,' said Caligula, and although it may be thought unfair to quote the words of an epileptic and a lunatic, history shows with hideous but fascinating clarity that in his time Caligula's outlook was not confined to one man, or even to a small circle. Everywhere we look we find the same thing. Roman society was based on slaves and these slaves were treated abominably, not only by their masters but by their mistresses as well; nor can this cruelty be explained away on the grounds of necessity, the different humanitarian conventions of past ages, or by anything else other than the simple and interesting truth. Juvenal attacks the sadism of women.

> But you should know what Everywoman does
> at home all day. Suppose her husband turns
> his back to her in bed. God help the housemaid!
> The lady's maids are stripped, the coachman's thrashed
> for being late (punished because another slept),
> rods are broken, bleeding backs are scourged
> and lashed: some women keep a private flogger.
> She scourges while her face is made up, talks
> to her friends, examines a gold-braided frock
> and thrashes, reads the daily paper through,
> and thrashes, til the thrasher tires, and she
> screams GO NOW, and the inquisition's over.
> She rules her home more savagely than a tyrant.

"In seeking the cause of a feature so prominent in a society, one naturally examines the system of education. Here, as elsewhere, we find the same old story, the frequent and severe floggings, the indoctrination in aggressive manhood which, as in the situation which was to echo it two thousand years later, could only lead to eventual misery for all concerned. But it is to be questioned whether these elements are not rather a mere result, a symptom of the original disease." [35]

A realization that this cruelty was in some way linked with sex must have dawned on certain of the Christian Fathers and probably added to the distrust they felt for sexual activities in general. St. Augustine, for one, clearly realized that the amphitheater, with its cruelties, did not encourage Christian behavior.

"A young Christian was living in Rome as a student. He had long avoided the amphitheater, but was at last taken to visit it by friends. He told them that they could drag his body there but not his soul, for he could sit with his eyes closed, and so be really absent. This he did, but a great shout induced him to open his eyes in curiosity. Then his soul was stricken more sorely than the bodies of those he yearned to see, and his fall was more lamentable than that which had caused the shout. For with the sight of blood he absorbed a lust for cruelty; he could not turn away; his gaze grew fixed; he was drunk with the lust for blood. Why should I say more? He looked, his blood burned, and he took away with him a madness which goaded him to return again."

The loathing they felt for these excesses of the pagan Romans, mingled with the distrust they felt for sexual indulgence and for worldly pleasure in general, caused the Fathers of the Church to create conditions in which the sickly Guilt Cult could arise and flourish.

ANTI-SEX AND THE CHURCH

The Jewish preoccupation with "impurity" carried over into Christianity in spite of the injunction given to Peter, "what God hath cleansed call not thou unclean." It did so gradually, just as a cancer, starting from a single malignant cell, may grow for years in the body without causing any outward manifestation of disease. In the Christianity of the first century A.D. we find little if any evidence of sex guilt. "What we find is numerous small congregations, trying to live in brotherly amity, but totally uninterested in the doctrine as we know it. They do not celebrate either the birth of Christ or his death as festivals; they do not claim that he was divine. (The divinity of Christ did not become official doctrine of the Church until A.D. 269 and then only over the protests of the patriarch of Samosata who said that it was nonsense.)" [28]

Nor, of course, did they claim that he was born of an immaculate conception, a claim which was not made until the second century. Augustine denied this story as late as the fifth century.

The central point of their gathering was not the celebration of the Eucharist, a ritual borrowed by St. Paul from the mystery religions, but the Agape, the "love feast," a real meal to which they brought real food. This Agape had little in common with the hymn and psalm routines decorously performed once a week in the meeting places of the more sedate Christian cults. They were lively, decidedly "Pentecostal" assemblies in which emphasis was placed on the immediate experience of the divinity. There were prophesyings and ecstasies, speaking in tongues, raptures and ravishings (spiritual variety). "There was, as it were, a liturgy of the Holy Spirit after the liturgy of Christ," writes Monsignor Duchesne, "a true liturgy with a real presence and communion. The inspiration could be felt; it sent a thrill through the organs of certain privileged persons; but the whole congregation was moved, edified and even more or less ravished by it and transported into the divine sphere of the Paraclete."

The raptures felt by these early brethren were not merely cerebral; the entire body participated in the uplift. Dancing, so frowned on by the later Fathers, was recognized as a means of approaching deeper experiences. "The dance," wrote Ambrose, "must in no wise be regarded as a mark of reverence for vanity and luxury, but as something which uplifts every living body instead of allowing the limbs to rest motionless on the floor or the slow feet to become numb." Jesus himself instituted this dancing, according to the Acts of John: "Jesus gathered us all together and bade us make a ring, holding one another's hands, and himself standing in the middle." The chant which accompanied the dance indicates that this exercise was thought of as a pathway to deeper understanding: "Who dances not knows not what will come to pass."

The purpose of these assemblies was to arouse that emotion which Paul praised so highly, without which all other spiritual gifts are worthless. "Though I speak with the tongues of men and of angels and have not love I am become as sounding brass or a tinkling cymbal."

Did the quest for this spiritual love rule out the manifestations of physical love? Was Eros necessarily regarded as the foe of Agape?

Paul had no doubt on this subject. Eros and Agape were not compatible. But in a world accustomed to bestow divine honors on both Eros and Aphrodite there were probably several Christian congregations who thought otherwise, for whom the rapture of sexual union seemed an aid, not a hindrance, in theoleptic experience.

Some time had to elapse before this primitive Christianity, with its emphasis on love and the direct experience of the Holy Spirit, became burdened with the cancerous Guilt Cult with its emphasis on sin, damnation and eternal fire. In the third and fourth century the development of this pathological growth took the form of monasticism, which, especially in Egypt, attained the status of a spiritual pestilence and irrevocably damaged the whole structure of the ancient civilization. The horror and disgust with which this movement was regarded by cultured Romans is well expressed by the comments of Rutilius Claudius Namantianus (c. A.D. 414). Speaking of the monks of Capri he exclaims: "The whole island is filled, or rather defiled, by men who fly from the light. They call themselves Monks or solitaries, because they choose to live alone, without any witnesses of their actions. They fear the gifts of fortune, from the apprehension of losing them; and, lest they should be miserable, they embrace a life of voluntary wretchedness. How absurd their choice! How perverse their understanding! To dread the evils without being able to support the blessings of the human condition. Either this melancholy madness is the effect of disease, or else the consciousness of guilt urges these unhappy men to exercise on their own bodies the tortures which are inflicted on fugitive slaves by the hand of justice."

The above passage from Gibbon's *Decline and Fall of the Roman Empire* is very instructive. Rutilius Namantianus could make no claim to what nowadays passes for scientific objectivity, but one observes how unerringly he classifies the monkish behavior pattern as a pathological state. A further quotation from Gibbon throws light on that weird sexual mixup which led to the concept of "brides of Christ," a concept which would doubtless have been as horrifying to the founder of Christianity as the burnings and torturings which the "faithful" so zealously applied in his name in a later age.

"The credulous maid was betrayed by vanity to violate the laws of nature: and the matron aspired to imaginary perfection, by renouncing the virtues of domestic life. Paula yielded to the persuasive eloquence of Jerome; and the profane title of mother-in-law of God tempted that illustrious widow to consecrate the virginity of her daughter Eustochium."

Mother-in-law of God! The mind reels before the vistas of celestial relationships here revealed. But the Fathers were not content with the mere imposition of celibacy. They thundered against sexuality itself, especially female sexuality. Jerome called woman *"saccus stercoris,"* a sack of filth, Tertullian called her a temple built over a sewer. Augustine called attention to the obscene commingling of the sexual and excretory organs, observing that all of us enter the world "between the feces and the urine." "Concupiscence is vice . . . human flesh born through it is a sinful flesh," wrote Augustine. "The union of the sexes transmits original sin to the child, being accompanied, since the Fall, by concupiscence."

Thus was the ground prepared for the emergence of the Guilt Cult in the Western world. Wrote Rattray Taylor: "Rape and incest characterize the sexual life of the English in the first millennium of our era; homosexuality and hysteria the years that followed. The Christian missionaries found a people who, especially in the Celtic parts of the country, maintained a free sexual morality. On them it sought to impose a code of extreme severity, and it steadily increased the strictness of its demands.

"The Church never succeeded in obtaining universal acceptance for its sexual regulations, but in time it became able to enforce sexual abstinence on a scale sufficient to produce a rich crop of mental disease. It is hardly too much to say that medieval Europe came to resemble a vast insane asylum." [28]

Many centuries were to pass before the Guilt Cult attained its greatest power. In England the hardy Celts were accustomed to a code of sexual behavior that did not draw the line even at incest. "They wear their hair long," wrote Julius Caesar of the ancient Britons, "and shave the whole of their bodies except the head and upper lip. Wives are shared between groups of ten or twelve men, especially between brothers and between fathers and sons; but the offspring of these unions are counted as the children of the man with whom a particular woman cohabited first." With such a tradition behind them the Celts resisted manfully the attempts of the Church to deprive them of their sexual liberties. The English, lamented Boniface in the eighth century, "utterly despise matrimony." He was filled with shame because they "utterly refuse to have legitimate wives and continue to live in lechery and adultery after the manner of neighing horses or braying asses." The negative teachings of the Church regarding sex were far from being accepted by these hearty Britons. Continence was considered by most people an unhealthy aberration and physicians were in the habit of recommending increased frequency of sexual intercourse to their patients as the method of relieving plethora. Both male and female nudity was accepted. The warriors had long been accustomed to fight naked; as for the women, they regarded it a mode of honoring a man to expose before him their private parts, as shown by the example of the Queen of Ulster and all the ladies of her court who came to meet Cuchulaine naked above the waist and raised their skirts to expose their sex organs.

And what of those gentle knights about whose antics such a web of romance has been woven, especially in connection with their gallantry toward women? If we overlook the drivelings of the sentimentalists and go back to the early historians we find them described as "Sanguinary, boastful, murderous, addicted to vice, adulterous and enemies of God . . . Although they keep large numbers of wives, they are fornicators and adulterers." "To judge from contemporary poems," wrote

Traill and Mann, "the first thought of every knight on finding a lady unprotected was to do her violence." Gawain, pattern of knighthood and courtesy, raped Gran de Lis despite her tears and screams. The hero of *Lai de Graelent* did the same thing to a lady he met in the forest. Malory informs us that when a knight entered the hall of King Arthur and carried off by force a weeping screaming woman "the king was glad, for she made such a noise."

Rape, however, was rarely necessary, for the ladies themselves as often as not made the advances and stated their propositions in the bluntest terms. It was a praiseworthy act to offer oneself to a valiant knight. Gawain praised the good taste of his own lady-love, Orgueilleuse, for having offered her favors to so valiant a warrior as the Red Knight. When a husband, in one of the Provençal romances, reproached his wife for her infidelity, she replied: "My Lord, you have no dishonor on that account, for the man I love is a noble baron, expert in arms, namely Roland, the nephew of King Charles." This reply not only silenced the husband but also filled him with confusion over his unseemly interference.

Marriage, far from being regarded as a sacred and indissoluble union, was treated as a temporary affair and frequent change of partners was usual until quite late in the Middle Ages. Bastardy, far from being regarded as a mark of shame, was regarded as a sign of distinction. The implication was that some knight of special valor had slept with one's mother. The Church did its best to impose monogamy as the decree of the Anglo-Saxon synod of 786 A.D. indicates: "We command then, in order to avoid fornication, that every layman shall have one legitimate wife and every woman one legitimate husband, in order that they may have and beget legitimate heirs according to God's law." It was a long while before these attempts succeeded. The ordinances of Howel the Good in the tenth century allowed seven-year trial marriages. In Scotland one-year trial marriage existed up to the Reformation.

By the twelfth century the gray clouds of the Guilt Cult

were gathering thickly over that segment of the human race which referred to itself collectively as "Christendom." The anti-Eros, a distorted and truly cloacal monster, bred in the sewers of the sacerdotal mind, manifested itself in the form of a series of edicts relating to every aspect of sexual life. These edicts took the form of penitential books and based all their pronouncements on an extraordinary premise. The sexual act is sinful. Desire for a person of the opposite sex, even if unconsummated, is sinful. And because the love of a man for a woman was held to be mere lust, it led to the incontrovertible proposition that no man should love his wife. It led Peter Lombard to write, in his pamphlet *De excusione coitus,* that for a man to love his wife is a sin worse than adultery.

Omnes ardentior amator propriae uxoris adulter est.

Let all who can follow the priestly example and observe complete celibacy. Virgins, virgins, virgins, let all remain virgins. The idea of virginity became an obsession. The Fathers had praised it. Saint Jerome had tolerated marriage only because it provided the world with potential virgins. And these virgins, by a twist of the imagination so amazing that it must make the contemporary biologist squirm, were converted into "Brides of Christ." From which it followed that anyone who seduced a virgin was not only committing fornication but also the more serious crime of adultery, adultery moreover at the expense of Christ! What crime more heinous! Comments Rattray Taylor: "The outraged deity was therefore entitled to the revenge which tradition has accorded to a husband in such a position. How literally this fantastic doctrine was held can be shown by a quotation from Cyprian: 'If a husband come and see his wife lying with another man, is he not indignant and maddened? . . . How indignant and angered then must Christ our Lord and Judge be, when He sees a virgin, dedicated to Himself, and consecrated to His holiness, lying with a man . . . She who has been guilty of this crime is an adulteress, not against a husband, but Christ.' Evidently the saint saw nothing ludicrous in the assumption that the Son of God would feel just the emotions of outraged property-sense which would be felt by the most boorish of human beings." [28]

Out of this mishmash of virulent nonsense there emerged a most peculiar code of sexual behavior. Fornication came to be defined as a worse sin than murder! Theodore and Bede imposed a penance for simple fornication of one year, a penalty which was increased according to the indiscretion of the parties. "Adultery was more serious than fornication with an unmarried person, and sexual connection with a monk or a nun more serious still. While if members of the clergy fornicated with a monk or nun, Dunstan's penalty was ten years' fast with perpetual lamentation and abstention from meat. Later the seducer was denied burial in consecrated ground."

From the standpoint of the irreverent modern the extremes to which the priests of the Guilt Cult went seem almost incredible. Not content with denying to mankind the simple joys of sexual intercourse they spread out their dark influence to cast a cloud even on masturbation. Homosexuality and bestiality were bad of course, but the sin on which the greatest emphasis was laid was masturbation! According to Aquinas it was a greater sin than fornication. In the five medieval penitential codes there are twenty-two paragraphs dealing with various degrees of sodomy and bestiality, and no fewer than twenty-five dealing with masturbation on the part of laymen, to say nothing of others dealing with masturbation on the part of clergy.

Even involuntary nocturnal pollution was a sin. The offender had to rise at once and sing seven penitential psalms and a further thirty in the morning. If pollution occurred when he had fallen asleep in church he had to sing the whole psalter.

The priests of the Guilt Cult admitted reluctantly that sexual intercourse between husband and wife was permissible but coitus from the rear was not admitted. The Church authorities termed it *"more canino,"* which is to say "dog fashion," and condemned it not because it degraded humans into the positions of beasts but because this mode of sexual intercourse was thought to be more pleasurable than the other. With such horror was this mode of intercourse regarded that those who indulged in it were penalized with seven years of penance.

Even the permissible face-to-face coitus was made as uninteresting as possible by the use of a special nightshirt, the *chemise cagoule,* which insulated the female body from any direct contact with that of the male but had in it one suitably placed hole through which the penis could be timidly protruded to perform its allowable work of generating new sinners for the Church to "save." But the frequency with which the operation could be performed was strictly limited. Intercourse was made illegal on Mondays, Wednesdays and Fridays, equivalent to five months out of twelve. Next it was made illegal for forty days before Easter and forty days before Christmas and three days before attending communion. It was forbidden from the time of conception to forty days after parturition and forbidden during any penance.

When one considers that the human female is only fertile for a relatively short period (about twenty-four hours after ovulation) it seems something of a miracle that any ova managed to get fertilized. And when one remembers that, in addition to all these sexual taboos, the population of Europe was scourged with disease, wasted with malnutrition, devastated with wars, it seems something of a wonder that the wretched continent managed to avoid becoming totally depopulated.

THE WITCH HYSTERIA

The dark ministers of the Guilt Cult were not satisfied with merely forbidding sexual indulgence. In the recesses of their diseased, fear-ridden minds a crop of monsters began to develop to which, with that lack of insight that is characteristic of the psychotic, they began to attribute objective existence. The monsters they created had their origins in the deities of the Ancient World, especially the varied followers of the great

Dionysus, nymphs, fauns, dryads, sileni, and the lascivious Pan. These imaginary entities were blended with the Greek concept of the *daimon,* a force which influenced individuals for good or ill. Out of these ingredients Gregory I composed a sort of synthetic devil with horns and hooves taken from Pan and the German forest sprites, a red beard and a smell derived from Thor, a limp from Vulcan or Wotan, black color from Saturn or Loki and power over the weather from Zeus or Wotan. This composite was described as "a pure spirit, dangerous and tempting but not the direct enemy of man."

Toward the end of the Middle Ages we find this generalized devil taking on a specifically sexual quality. In a bull issued by Pope Innocent VIII mention is made of persons who have abandoned themselves to devils, incubi and succubi, thereby attaining the power, among other things, of hindering men "from performing the sexual act and women from conceiving, whence husbands cannot know their wives, nor wives receive their husbands . . ." The statement is extraordinary for its lack of logic. It attributes to devils the power to enforce that very condition (sexual abstinence) that the Church itself had striven so earnestly to impose. But Popes are infallible where matters of doctrine are concerned, and therefore do not need to be logical. The devil, so the Pope himself decreed, must henceforth be regarded as a person, not a mere symbol of error. His anatomy was accurately described, special attention being devoted to his penis, always of enormous size and often forked, as is the penis of some snakes, which enabled him to penetrate a woman by the vagina and anus simultaneously. Serving this picturesque monstrosity was a host of lesser devils including the incubi which were male and the succubi which were female.

The total number of the devil's employees was calculated to be 7,405,926. His dominion, hell, was carefully depicted and equipped with topography, flora, fauna and climate. The learned Jesuit Cornelius Lapide calculated that hell was two hundred Italian miles across, a modest domain yet adequate, for a German theologian had decided that one cubic mile was sufficient to contain one hundred billion souls, provided they were packed tightly, "like anchovies."

So the Guilt Cult now had its devil and proceeded to lavish on this creation a degree of attention that it had never devoted to God. The high priests of the cult were the German inquisitors Kramer and Sprenger. These two members of the Dominican order, activated by a twisted sexuality which saw evil in every erotic manifestation, lavished on the human female the hatred generated within them by enforced celibacy. In the *Malleus Maleficarum*, most influential of the books on witchcraft, responsible for the agony and death of thousands, they expressed their loathing of woman in general. ". . . she is an imperfect animal, she always deceives . . . All witchcraft comes from carnal lust, which is in woman insatiable. Wherefore for the sake of fulfilling their lusts they consort even with devils."

As late as 900 A.D. the Church had specifically denied the possibility of sexual intercourse between humans and supernatural beings. Kramer and Sprenger changed all that and dragged the Church with them into that hideous jungle of delusions that their own misdirected sex energy had created. It was the fateful bull of Innocent VIII, issued in 1484, that let loose these maniacs on society and provided justification for the orgy of legalized murder that lasted into the nineteenth century (a witch was consigned to the flames in Peru as late as 1888). About this R. E. L. Masters writes as follows:

"It is true that Protestants, too, burned witches. However, they did not contribute much of importance to the theory and trappings of witchcraft, merely taking over in the main the ideas and practices of the Inquisition. Almost the entire blame for the hideous nightmare that was the witch mania, and the greatest part of the blame for poisoning the sexual life of the West, rests squarely upon the Roman Catholic Church." [46]

Space does not permit a full account of the sexual delusions that plagued alike the witch-hunters and those they accused. The inquisitors seized on the fantasies of schizophrenics and hysterics, added to these their own fears and obsessions, built up a gruesome feed-back system in which terror amplified terror, delusion bred delusion, until no one from the highest to the lowest could remain unaffected. All the inquisitors worked with an interrogatory or manual of questions and, as these questions were almost wholly sexual, they generally succeeded in finding sexual guilt. The black-robed celibates projected upon the accused all the sexual fantasies that cluttered their own guilt-ridden minds. "Practically all of us are capable of practically anything," wrote Aldous Huxley in his study of demonology (*The Devils of Loudon*).[47] And so these inquisitors, ministers of a Guilt Cult which had done its best to poison Eros, found themselves victims of the love god's vengeance, haunted by hideous fantasies in which all the beauty and creativity of sex was converted to ugliness and filth.

That this loathsome cult had nothing whatever to do with the teachings of Jesus need hardly be pointed out here. The Christian churches, with a few honorable exceptions, have never had much use for the sacred teachings offered to his chosen disciples by the Galilean Initiate. They installed, in place of the loving Redeemer who had dined with sinners, forgiven a prostitute and stood up for a woman taken in adultery, a cruel narrow-minded fanatic, obsessed with ideas of vengeance and surrounded with hell-fire. In short they abandoned Jesus and worshipped a devil of their own creating. They projected that devil into the minds of others, then used this as an excuse to gratify their appetite for tormenting their fellow men and especially fellow women. They employed in this activity the sex energy that they would not allow to flow in its normal channels.

"Predictably, those who hated the flesh became obsessed by the flesh. Inquisitors and others who dealt with witches doted upon every erotic detail of the confessions and testimony, encouraged the morbid and the sensational, examined naked witches for the Devil's Mark (shaving their bodies the better to find it), and in all displayed such shameless avidity in matters erotic as to provoke public criticism.

"The Devil's Mark, which often resembled the foot of a hare or of a toad, was believed placed by Him on the flesh of each witch so that the witch could not attempt later to deny that a pact had been made. It was often concealed in the female genitals and in the rectum, and was anesthetic. To make certain that some blemish was in fact the Devil's Mark, long pins would be inserted into the flesh of the witch. One may well imagine that sadists were attracted to the work of driving pins into the breasts and genitalia and other sensitive body parts of witches." [46]

The destructive orgy reached incredible proportions. In Bamberg between 1609 and 1633 nine hundred persons were burned including the burgomaster Johannes Junius, who wrote to his daughter: "It is all falsehood and invention. They never cease the torture until one says something." According to Lea, a bishop of Geneva burned five hundred in three months, a bishop of Wirzburg nine hundred. Eight hundred were condemned in a single body by the senate of Savoy. In a century and a half from 1404 to 1554 the Holy Office burned at least thirty thousand witches.

SEX AND PAIN

The destructive excesses of the inquisitors and witch-hunters are extreme examples of the negative force that seems to be a part of human sexuality. Biologically speaking it is evident that pain, fear and sexual excitation are linked in some way. The link between pain and sexual excitement is attested to by the popularity of flagellation. "There are some nations," wrote Paulini in *Flagellium Salutarius* (1698), "particularly the Persians and the Russians, where the women regard a whipping as a peculiar sign of love and favor. The Russian women are never more pleased and delighted than when they receive such attentions from their husbands. A German who went to Russia took a Russian wife to whom he was always kind in everything. But she always wore an expression of dissatisfaction and went about with sighs and downcast eyes. The husband asked the reason, for he could not understand what was wrong. He embraced her and begged to be told what he had carelessly done to hurt her feelings. 'I want nothing,' was the answer, 'but what is customary in our country—the whip, the real sign of love.' When he adopted this custom his wife began to love him dearly. Similar stories are told by Peter Petreus of Erlesund, who adds that husbands, immediately after the wedding, among other indispensable household articles, provide themselves with a whip."

This mode of sexual gratification was enormously encouraged by the Church's negative attitude toward sex. Flagellation had the advantage of offering a sexual outlet which could be conveniently disguised as a penance. Several nuns, Maria Magdalena of Pazzi and Elizabeth of Genton in particular, were aroused to such states of excitation by whipping that even the coldest clerics marveled. Maria of Pazzi, a Carmelite nun in Florence (1580), became quite celebrated. Her greatest delight was to have her hands bound by the prioress behind her back and her naked buttocks whipped in the presence of the assembled sisters. While being whipped her thoughts were of love. The inner fire threatened to consume her and she frequently cried, "Enough! Fan no longer the flame that consumes me. This is not the death I long for. It comes with all too much pleasure and delight."

It was the same, Krafft-Ebing informs us, with Elizabeth of Genton. As a result of whipping she passed into a state of bacchanalian madness. Excited by flagellation she believed herself united with her "idea." This condition was so exquisitely pleasant that she would frequently cry out: "O love, O eternal love. O love, O you creatures! cry out with me: 'Love, Love.'"

The practice of flagellation was by no means confined to nuns. As the Guilt Cult poisoned Eros these manifestations became rampant throughout Europe. Flagellants were said at one time to number eight hundred thousand in France alone. The practice was not confined to France but spread rapidly, extending as far as the Rhine provinces, across Germany and into Bohemia. Like the worshippers of Cybele described by Apuleius, these victims of sexual guilt would scourge themselves until their bodies ran with blood. Day and night, long processions of all classes and ages, headed by priests carrying crosses and banners, perambulated the streets in double file reciting prayers and briskly scourging themselves. So widespread did the cult become that even the Church, the antisexual teachings of which were directly responsible for these manifestations, became alarmed. In 1349 Clement VI pronounced flagellation to be a heresy.

Heresy or not, it continued to flourish. Later it lost its religious overtones as the power of the Guilt Cult declined. Instead it became a form of erotic experience. Clubs were formed to ensure that the art of flagellation would not be lost. The *Bon Ton* magazine of December, 1792, describes the procedure used in one such club, the membership of which was entirely female.

"These female members are mainly married women, who, tired of marriage in its usual form, and the cold indifference which is wont to accompany it, determined by a novel method to reawaken the ecstasy which they knew at the beginning of their married life . . . The honorable society or club to which we refer never has fewer than twelve members. At each meeting six are chastised by the other six. They draw lots for the order of procedure: then, either a written speech is read, describing flagellation as it has been practiced from the earliest age up to the present day . . . after which the six patients take their places, and the six flagellants begin the practical demonstration. The president of the club hands to each a stout rod, and begins the chastisement herself, with any variation she likes, while the others watch. Sometimes, by order of the president, the whipping starts on the calves and goes up to the posterior, until the whole region, as Shakespeare says, from milk-white 'becomes one red.' "

The male is often just as reactive to this form of stimulation as is the female. "*Libido sexualis*," wrote Krafft-Ebing primly, "may also be induced by stimulation of the gluteal regions (castigation, whipping) . . . It sometimes happens that in boys the first excitation of the sexual instinct is caused by a spanking." This seems especially true when the punishment is administered by a female. This manifestation of sex energy was especially prevalent in England during the eighteenth century; indeed the male need for physical chastisement at the hands of the female was so acute that several astute females made a fortune by supplying what these gentlemen so earnestly required. One such was Mrs. Theresa Berkeley who, at her home at 28 Charlotte Street, Portland Place, made 10,000 pounds in eight years and lived in luxury the while. "Her arsenal of implements was immensely more complete than that of any other governess . . . In her establishment anyone provided with reasonable means could have himself beaten with canes, scourges, whips and straps; pricked with needles, half-strangled, scrubbed with many kinds of harsh brushes, scourged with nettles, currycombed, bled and tortured until he had had enough of it." [48]

This form of sexual arousal has retained its popularity in England. "Until recently you could see the ads in Soho shop windows," writes Wayland Young of contemporary London. " 'Miss Du Sade; Miss Du Cane; Miss De Belting (Flagellation), Strict governess: Corrective Training; Corr. and Disc. (the sado-masochistic procedures in general).' The price was a pound a stroke (either way). Sometimes the girls would get carried away by their enthusiasm.

" ' So then I gave him the three he'd paid for. But I don't know what it was; I was just feeling like it, I suppose, but I suddenly lost my temper, oh, not only with him, with everything and everybody. So I gave him four more and took another four quid off him and chucked him out. I really lit into him; he loved it. And people ask me why I like cats.' " [49]

SADE AND THE SADISTS

The link that exists between pain and Eros is biologically valid up to a point. As the sage Vatsyayana observes: "Two lovers in the heat and sweat of excitement are blinded by mutual passion and pursue their mad course of pleasure with fury and without regard for the excesses that many commit during the act." [50] Such excesses may take the form of slaps, bitings, scratchings and even moderate flagellation and still be considered within the bounds of normality. But there are limits, and when these limits are passed we enter the realm of pathology, of sex energy degraded. So, speaking of the cruel excesses prevalent in certain parts of India of his day (third or fourth century A.D.), Vatsyayana states: "The use of instruments is peculiar to people from the south and one can see the scars left by these objects on the breasts and bodies of the women of these lands. These ways of lovemaking are peculiar to certain localities, but Vatsyayana is of the opinion that these methods are dangerous, painful and barbarous, and should not be imitated."

Such wise moderation was rejected by certain deranged spirits in the West who, taking their cue from the witch-burners and inquisitors, continued the work of converting Eros into a demon. During the eighteenth century both in England and in Continental Europe, degradation of sex energy took the form of a mania for defloration and for sexual assault of girls below the age of puberty.

The trade in virgins continued well into the nineteenth century, the traffic being fostered by the antisexual obsession that dominated England during that period. Girls of good family

were tricked by offers of positions, then sold to brothel keep-
ers, chiefly in Belgium, from whose clutches they rarely escaped alive. "It was in the 1850's," writes Terrot in *Traffic in
Innocents*,[51] "that the demands of the Continental market
began to grow more exacting. Accordingly their British agents
turned their attention to higher classes of the community, particularly to middle-class families who were living beyond their
means. To their own intense astonishment they obtained such
a plentiful supply of girls from this class that before long they
almost ceased operations in the industrial areas . . . The principal reason for their success lies in a bald statement written
by a French police officer in 1859: 'The education of English
girls is usually of such a strictly prudish character, that in their
simplicity and ignorance of the world they offer themselves the
easiest prey imaginable.'"

The passion for defloration of virgins sometimes took exotic
forms, as evidenced by the "Feast of Venus" celebrated at the
house of Charlotte Hayes in London in front of an audience
which, according to Bloch, consisted mainly of impotent de-
bauchees who required every possible stimulation for the satisfaction of their lusts. The "Feast of Venus" was based on a
description which Hawksworth, traveling companion of Captain Cook, had made of the public defloration of young girls
on the island of Tahiti. Hawksworth was present at such a
ceremony and related that girls of eleven were publicly
mounted and deflowered by powerful young men in the presence of the chiefs and elders from whom they received detailed advice on sexual technique.

The ceremony was performed for a very different purpose
at the establishment of Charlotte Hayes, its aim being to provide titillation for elderly customers who, having lost the
power to deflower virgins themselves, had to obtain satisfaction from watching others perform this operation. Accordingly,
"at 7 o'clock precisely," as stated in the advertisement, "twelve
beautiful nymphs, spotless virgins," were ceremoniously
mounted by twelve lusty youths before the eyes of an en-

tranced audience which included five members of the House of Commons. After this a sumptuous meal was taken." [51]

This impulse to degrade sex energy found its most extreme literary expression in the writings of Donatien Alphonse François de Sade. The Marquis made several serious attempts to practice what he preached. He whipped a woman, Rose Keller, on Easter day, 1769, and threatened to murder her. He held parties at which candies treated with cantharides (Spanish fly) were served to the guests, as a result of which, according to one observer, "all those who had eaten it, burning with unchaste desire, gave themselves up to all the excesses to which the most lascivious frenzy can carry one." Such excesses brought De Sade into trouble with the law and resulted in his imprisonment in the Bastille where he occupied himself with setting down on paper the fantasies that obsessed him.

There has been some effort of late to represent Sade as a genuine philosopher with a message of a sort. His works are now available in English and can be read by anyone rich enough to afford them. They are of interest only to students of the anti-Eros and to those who happen to share Sade's diseased tastes. As a writer the man is a crushing bore, verbose, elaborate, tiresome and unskillful. He presents the anti-Eros in all its twisted ugliness, piling excess on excess, until the reader hesitates between feelings of ridicule and disgust. His "heroes" are outcasts from society, ogrelike monstrosities who live in castles, underground palaces, secret hideouts, guarded from the inroads of the law. They are usually exceedingly rich. They are equipped, in many cases, with a sexual apparatus so absurdly overdeveloped that no normal anatomy could even support the monstrous excrescence. (Roland, in *Justine*, had a penis "of such huge size that it was wholly certain that Nature had never made anything so prodigious. Both my hands hardly went round it, and it was as long as from my elbow to my wrist.")

These monstrously equipped madmen had one aim only: to degrade, torture and mutilate members of the opposite sex.

The accounts of assaults and tortures, flagellations and coprophagy are interspersed with discourses termed by the author "philosophical," the gist of which is that nature is herself a criminal force. Therefore it behooves man to act as criminally as possible and thereby to imitate nature.

De Sade's characters move like mechanical dolls against the Gothic background of dungeons, whips, instruments of torture. They never attain even a semblance of humanity. Both the "virtue" of Justine and the "vice" of Juliette have a synthetic quality. The assaults suffered by Justine would infallibly have produced fatal injuries and the girl would have died after the first five chapters, yet she survives and seems not much the worse even when beaten with an iron hammer equipped with spikes which caused her blood to spurt to the ceiling. The whole story deteriorates into a catalogue of absurdities.

Much the same can be said of a recent variation on the De Sade theme, appropriately named *The Story of O*. The name is appropriate because O is a cipher. She obviously does not, probably could not, exist. She is, we are informed, a representative of a kind of woman who delights in slavery. In the course of satisfying this delight she gives herself totally to her "lover," René, who duly hands her over to a group of torturers by whom she is whipped, sodomized, branded with a hot iron on her buttocks, all of which she suffers without complaint. The torments are not even inflicted by the so-called lover, but by various anonymous characters or by a phony English aristocrat called "Sir Stephen." From time to time René the lover pops up like a mechanical doll and says, "I love you." Then he hands O over again to her tormentors.

Such works as *Justine, Juliette* and *The Story of O* emphasize the chief characteristic of the anti-Eros. This consists in a failure to use the energy of sex as a means of breaking out of one's personal prison and attaining union, however brief, with another being. The disease is due, in part, to cerebral sex. The sufferer can never let go or allow himself to be overwhelmed by his own bodily sensations. ". . . Desire and pleasure explode in furious attacks upon this cold, tense body, proof against all enchantment. They do not constitute a living experience within the framework of the subject's psycho-physiological unity. Instead they blast him, like some kind of bodily accident." [52]

The victim of the anti-Eros is thus never able to attain satisfaction through normal sexual union. Desperately striving for release he seeks more and more violent methods. Pleasant sensations are all too mild. Normal love involves sharing pleasure with another, which the victim of the anti-Eros, locked in the prison of his egotism, refuses to do. So he seeks release in the most violent of experiences. As Sade puts it, "No kind of sensation is keener and more active than that of pain; its impressions are unmistakable . . . It is simply a matter of jangling all our nerves with the most violent possible shock. Now, since there can be no doubt that pain affects us more strongly than pleasure, when this sensation is produced in others, our very being will vibrate more vigorously with the resulting shocks."

It is quite evident that, in those who suffer from this disease, sex energy flows in nervous channels directly connected to those centers in the brain which generate rage and cruelty. Sade's description of the Duke of Blangis in the throes of orgasm illustrates the consequences of such abnormal neurological connections. "Horrible shrieks and dreadful oaths escaped his heaving breast. Flames seemed to dart from his eyes. He frothed at the mouth, he whinnied . . ." After which we are hardly surprised to learn that he terminated the act by strangling his partner.

OBSCENITY AND PORNOGRAPHY

One of the strangest by-products of the anti-Eros was the concept of obscenity which developed in certain countries in the West and which, despite a weakening of the power of the Guilt Cult, continues to be taken seriously both in Britain and in the United States. To a cynical biologist few events seem more comical than the so-called obscenity trials which occur from time to time and involve some book or other in the pages of which the process of copulation has been described or depicted. The comedy results from the anguished efforts of learned jurists, all the way up to the Supreme Court, to define that which is indefinable—and of members of juries all over the country to interpret the rulings of these jurists.

The concept of obscenity is a by-product of mammalian anatomy. As was mentioned earlier, if man resembled the snail and had the organ of copulation in his head, far from the defiling presence of feces and urine, the idea of sex being in some way unclean would not have arisen. But the anatomical peculiarities of the vertebrates, all of which use the same openings for excretion and products of the sex glands, would not by themselves have created the idea of obscenity had not the Guilt Cult started its campaign against sex and tried to poison Eros and Aphrodite. Cultures with a normal attitude toward sex found it perfectly possible to venerate sex energy and saw nothing obscene in covering their temples with sculptured representations of sexual unions like those which cover the temple of the sun at Konarak in India.

The word most frequently met with in obscenity trials is "filth." This was well illustrated by the emphasis placed on the "two enormous turds" which appear at one point in Henry Miller's *Tropic of Cancer*. In the course of various trials in which sellers of this book were prosecuted those turds became symbolic. It is well known that everyone produces turds, indeed a failure to do so is just cause for alarm. Large sums of money are spent on advertisements of remedies for those who fail to produce turds in sufficient amount and with sufficient regularity. Nevertheless a jury of four men and eight women were solemnly sworn to decide, at considerable cost in public money and personal inconvenience to the jurors, whether those "two enormous turds" were to be considered "obscene."

The need to make this brain-twisting decision confronted twelve citizens of Marin County, California, in a trial begun on December 5, 1961, that lasted until December 15. The turds were finally acquitted and so was the book dealer who had dared to sell a book in which they were mentioned to the citizens of Marin County who presumably were not supposed to know about such things.

The muddle into which this obscenity concept has led even the highest authorities was shown during a recent trial which occupied no less a body than the Supreme Court of the United States. In this trial, surely one of the strangest in recent times, a certain Ralph Ginzberg was sentenced for five years to a Federal prison. He was punished not for writing about anything as factual as two enormous turds but for advertising his magazine *Eros* in such a way as to make it appear erotically arousing. "The leer of the sensualist," wrote Justice Brennan, "permeates the advertising of the three publications." But if sensual advertising is to be penalized surely half the inhabitants of Madison Avenue would be in jail!

The ruling evoked vigorous dissent from many people, including four Supreme Court justices. It focused a glaring light on the almost hopeless mixup that prevails in this area of legislation. The Supreme Court itself had tried to provide the guidelines. Material can be found obscene only if it is (a) "utterly without redeeming social importance," (b) if its dominant theme, taken as a whole, appeals to prurient interest in the "average" person (who is an average person?), (c) if it is "patently offensive because it affronts contemporary community standards" (which community? New York City? the Ozarks? the Deep South? the Middle West?).

All of which is bad enough, but the Ginzberg decision suggests that the Supreme Court justices abandoned even these shadowy guides. This was the impression received by one of the dissenting justices. "What I fear the Court has done today," said Justice Harlan, "is in effect to write a new statute, but

without the sharply focused definitions and standards necessary in such a sensitive area."

Can definitions and standards ever be sharply focused in this
"sensitive area"? Are all the attempts of the moralist to define
obscenity as futile as the efforts of the hunters of the Snark,
"a mythological animal of ill-defined characteristics." What is
a reasonable biologist to make of a pronouncement, solemnly
reported in *Time* magazine, in connection with a movie called
Caprice: " 'A brief shot of a male derrière is not going to present a problem to a normal individual,' he said. 'But exposure
of the female rear,' added Father Sullivan, 'is pruriently stimulating.' " Which female rear? Pruriently stimulating for whom?
And why should it be considered "prurient" for a human male
to take an interest in a female bottom? And how is the Reverend Patrick J. Sullivan to decide how the male will react to
this visual stimulation?

An impartial biologist, surveying this mess of foggy definitions, sweeping generalizations, assumptions unsupported by
scientific evidence, might sincerely advise the lawmakers to
extricate themselves from this morass and let people read or
look at whatever they please. After all, as Justice William
Douglas observed: ". . . judges cannot gear the literary diet
of an entire nation to whatever tepid stuff is incapable of
triggering the most demented mind." Nevertheless there is one
type of writing that can, with a fair degree of precision, be
defined not as obscene (a wretched little word practically
devoid of meaning) but as sexually pathological and therefore liable to incite to crimes of violence with sexual motivation.

That such literature should be placed out of reach of the
general reader was suggested recently by Pamela Hansford
Johnson whose book, *On Iniquity*,[53] was inspired by nagging
thoughts that followed her study of the "moors murders" case,
a particularly revolting example of sexual crime that occurred
in England in 1965. Her book is aimed at "the all-permissive,
the 'swinging society' under its Big Top, the whole garish

circus of the new freedom, freedom to revel—through all kinds of mass media—in violence, in pornography, in sado-masochism." This writer raised something of a storm by protesting, in a letter to *The Guardian,* against the availability of Krafft-Ebing's *Psychopathia Sexualis* in a cheap paperback on the bookstalls of English railway stations. Defending her position she writes: "There are some books that are not fit for all people and some people who are not fit for all books." She admits that no one can prove a causal connection between what the murderers read and what they did, but she adds: "I cannot help but wonder whether, by making all books available to all men, we do not pay too high a price, if that price should be the death of one small child by torture."

Whether or not one agrees with this conclusion, he who advocates the suppression of pathological sex literature for the reason that it degrades Eros is at least on fairly firm biological ground. Such literature encourages the diversion of sex energy, the joyous life-giving force, into dark and dangerous channels, a diversion that may very well result in the actualization of the kind of destructive orgies described ad nauseam in Sade's novels. All this black literature, the literature of the anti-Eros, is comparable to a reservoir of disease, a disease which might be regarded as contagious. Legislation designed to protect the weak and impressionable from contact with these pathological ideas might be justified on the grounds that what Sade and Company are advocating is criminal activity in the fullest sense of the word.

Such legislation, although admirably motivated and biologically justifiable, would probably not be effective even if passed. For one thing, the lawmakers, to be consistent, would have to ban not only books describing sexually motivated violence but violence of all kinds. It is manifestly absurd to prohibit books dealing with sexual violence when every child is exposed to an endless exhibition of nonsexual violence, murder, torture, mayhem of all kinds via various comic books or television.

Furthermore, one school of thought maintains that pathogenic literature of the Sade variety, far from leading its readers to enact the crimes described, actually drains off the dangerous energies and dissipates them in fantasies which, however lurid, at least do not harm anyone else. The Kronhausens, in *Pornography and the Law*,[54] express this point of view. "We believe that it is clinically very dangerous to block by critical or prohibitory attitudes and actions the few remaining fantasy outlets of sexually disturbed individuals." It is, in any case, practically impossible to control this kind of literature and suppression tends to make it more exciting by developing around it the aura of the forbidden.

EBB OF THE TIDE?

It is generally agreed that, in the Western world, the gray flood of the Guilt Cult has at last begun to recede. The forms of Eros and Aphrodite, for so long covered in slime, have begun to emerge again into the light of day. They are still partly coated in mud but at least they have become visible. Some might even insist that they have become too visible, that from having been absurdly sex-repressed we have now become sex-obsessed and are placing on this biological function more emphasis than it has any right to receive.

Actually Western society has yet to come to terms with the god and goddess of sexual love. The Guilt Cult is still a destructive force in society, imposing irrational and unbiological forms of behavior, standing in the way of real sexual enlightenment. A few items will illustrate its vast power of unreason.

Item: A sixteen-year-old girl, mother already of three illegitimate children, was instructed by her own mother in the techniques of contraception. Did a grateful society present Mom with a bouquet for striving to halt this orgy of immature maternity? Not at all. She was hauled into court for "contributing to the delinquency of a minor." This happened in the supposedly enlightened state of Illinois.

Item: An official, appalled by the black tide of illegitimate Negro babies swallowing relief funds in the city of Chicago, recommended distribution of contraceptive information and material. Did the grateful taxpayers present this thoughtful official with a medal? Not at all. He was fired from his job. The flood of black babies continued unchecked.

Item: A California housewife, shocked by the frequency of pregnancies among girls in high school, undertook personally to educate the male adolescents in the art of properly controlled sexual intercourse. Was she praised for this effort to fill one of the most obvious gaps in the contemporary program of education? Far from it. She too was hauled into court on the charge of contributing to the delinquency of a minor. Meanwhile the number of high-school pregnancies continued to rise.

Item: A university biologist commented on the sex life of the students: "With modern contraceptives and medical advice readily available at the nearest drugstore or at least a family physician, there is no valid reason why sexual intercourse should not be condoned among those sufficiently mature to engage in it without violating their own codes of morality and ethics." Was a prize awarded to the professor for making so sensible a statement? Far from it. Out of the local jungles emerged a devotee of the Guilt Cult snorting hell-fire and righteous indignation. "Standard operating procedure of the Communist conspiracy to demoralize a nation . . ." (One notes that Communism has now replaced the Devil as the major sexual threat.) A hundred hysterical parents, frightened by these denunciations, clamored for the professor's dismissal. Did the president of the university boldly stand up for academic freedom and the right of a biologist to express himself on matters biological? Not at all. He sided with the devotees of the Guilt Cult. The professor was fired.

One could continue ad nauseam and almost ad infinitum to catalogue these absurdities. Although the way to sane sexual behavior has been opened by modern science, members of contemporary society refuse to take it, muddled by the old fears and falsehoods, by endless "thou shalt nots" left over from a previous age. Despite the labors of the liberators a tangled mass of hypocrisy, misinformation, guilt, confusion, fear and sheer stupidity surrounds the subject of what is and what is not permissible in patterns of sexual behavior. And the devotees of the Guilt Cult, smugly convinced that their every utterance represents the word of God, continue their valiant efforts to drag their fellow citizens back into the dark ages of sexual repression.

We quote once more Nietzsche's saying: "Christianity poisoned Eros." In place of the triumphant phallus, symbol of life renewed and sexual joy, it erected an instrument of torture and death, a means of execution so degrading that even the brutal Romans reserved it only for foreigners or slaves. "What a bloodthirsty, violent religion yours must be, with that tortured man suspended from two pieces of wood on every altar." [55] This comment by a cultured Japanese expresses the natural reaction of any intelligent human being to the hideous object which Christianity has selected as its sacred symbol. Worship a cross? One might as well bow down to the gallows, the guillotine, the electric chair, the rack or the whipping post. No wonder preoccupation with guilt, sin, shame, death, punishment, hell-fire and everlasting torture almost completely eliminated the original teaching of love and forgiveness. The Good Shepherd was converted into a monster who would roast his sheep alive eternally for the slightest offense. It was this monster, the creation of a celibate priesthood maddened by their own frustrated desires, that gave to Eros that poison from the effects of which he still suffers.

Our "sexual revolution," as Dr. Benjamin Morse has called it, has certainly freed many people from the phantoms that haunted their grandparents. But it has failed to restore to us the joyous Dionysian attitude toward sexual phenomena that characterized the peoples of the Ancient World. Our attitude toward sex is chilly and cerebral, "sicklied o'er with the pale cast of thought." The young, if they are instructed in the mysteries of love at all, learn not in the sacred temples of Eros or Aphrodite from priests and priestesses skilled in all aspects of the art of love but from chilly little books on "sexual hygiene," written by tired M.D.'s in a style as uninspiring as that of an income tax form. Our sex lives, such as they are, are probed by the long thin fingers of sexologists who confront us, glassy-eyed with scientific objectivity, to inquire how often, when, where and in what postures we have intercourse, do we or do we not regularly attain an orgasm and were we or were we not in the habit of coupling with dumb beasts during our adolescence back on the farm.

These studies, cold, unbiased, impersonal and statistical must be welcomed by the scientist as evidence of the approach of a more *sensible* attitude toward sex. But there is something about all those graphs and tables which play so large a part in the massive *Kinsey Report* that strikes a chill. It is so totally un-Dionysian, so utterly remote from the raptures, the ecstasies, the orgies that ancient peoples associated with the phallic and cunnic sexual deities. Our love-locked panting couples are here observed in their vibrant embrace by an ex-entomologist with the cool objectivity of a student of solitary wasps. Such a chilly survey would frighten even the gods.

> When Kinsey dawned upon the scene
> Venus turned blue and Eros green
> And Pans and nymphs in trembling droves
> Fled howling from the sacred groves;
> Seeing our sexual ballistics
> Frozen in ranks of cold statistics
> And our most frenzied copulations
> Transmuted into mere equations.

Similarly Drs. Masters and Johnson, whose courage in embarking on a study of the physiology of human sex cannot be praised too highly, might cause the love gods to shudder by their clinical approach. The subjects of this research, we are assured, "felt secure in their surroundings and confident of their ability to perform. They rapidly gained confidence in their ability to respond successfully while subjected to a variety of recording techniques." Perhaps . . . And perhaps this cool clinical approach is just what we need to rout the still entrenched forces of the Guilt Cult and initiate a sane program of sexual education both for the young and the not so young. Yet one may wonder whether the reactions of a woman kneeling in the knee-chest position and being penetrated by an artificial phallus of transparent plastic activated by an electric motor, closely observed the while by an attendant gynecologist, are really representative of the normal female sexual response. And are we being sloppy and romantic if we admit that the thought of this operation strikes a certain chill, despite (or perhaps because of) the complete objectivity of the research personnel?

This clinical attitude toward sex has infected our writers and even the poets. Though novels and verses drip and ooze with sex, from Ginsberg's "Howl" to Miller's *Tropic*, not one recaptures the Dionysian frenzy. Their maenads croak, their satyrs creak, their tiresome anti-heroes and blowsy anti-heroines copulate wearily in a miasma of smegma and stale sweat. Or else, like Lady Chatterley and her gamekeeper, seem lapped in the odor of carbolic soap.

If any writer of our modern age can claim to have restored to the sexual function something of its pagan splendor, mystery and freedom from sentimentality it is Lawrence Durrell. Posing his great archetypes against the towers and minarets of an Alexandria as mythical as they are, Durrell has engaged in "a continuing investigation of modern love" (to quote from the jacket of the paperback edition). Certainly he shows us plenty of love, squared love, crossed love, love in the mist, the sand, the sea, love by candlelight, starlight, corpse-light, hell-fire and shell-fire. This love is always portrayed as a phantom receding, a vision uncaptured, a dream of perfection that is somehow never perfected.

Where in all this welter of copulation is the ultimate revelation, the searing flash of Dionysian insight? Among the intertwined lovers one seeks it in vain. Darley on Melissa, on Justine, on the long-haired Clea, Justine on Nessim, Pursewarden on Melissa or his sister Liza, Mountolive on Leila, Balthazar with his Ganymede, none provides a genuine glimpse of the sacred fire.

One is left with an uneasy suspicion that the final word on this subject that Durrell can offer is contained in a devastating passage in *Justine*.[25] It shows us the writer-schoolmaster Darley walking the streets of Alexandria on a summer night. This Darley, bold fellow, had taken the bull by the horns or the phallus by the shaft, telling himself, "I want to know what it really means," referring to "the whole portentous scrimmage of sex itself."

So what does it really mean? Detached as the aseptic research personnel of the Reproductive Biology Research Foundation, Darley surprised in the copulatory act a coarse hairy couple in a sleazy cubicle fitfully lighted by a buzzing paraffin lamp. To get the full impact of this discovery one must quote the original:

"They lay there like the victims of some terrible accident, clumsily engaged as if in some incoherent experimental fashion they were the first partners in the history of the human race to think out this peculiar means of communication. Their posture, so ludicrous and ill planned, seemed the result of some early trial which might, after centuries of experiment, evolve into a disposition of bodies as breathlessly congruent as a ballet position. But nevertheless I recognized that this had been fixed immutably, for all time, this eternally tragic and ludicrous position of engagement. From this sprang all those aspects of love which the wit of the poets and madmen used to elaborate their philosophy of fine obstructions. From this point the sick, the insane started growing; and from here too the disgusted and dispirited faces of the long-married, tied to each other back to back, so to speak, like dogs unable to disengage after coupling."

"Eternally tragic . . . a ludicrous position of engagement"—this from Durrell whom no one can call a prude. And it was Durrell, through the mouth of Pursewarden, who reproached D. H. Lawrence for erecting a Taj Mahal over anything as simple as a good fuck. The disenchantment is everywhere. The inhabitants of Durrell's Alexandria are as far away in spirit as they are in space-time from those of the Alexandria of Ptolemy Philadelphus who greeted with such religious enthusiasm the monstrous phallus that that enlightened ruler caused to be carried through the streets. It is hard to avoid the conclusion that the age of religious sexual enthusiasm is over. The malignant dualism, product of the Guilt Cult, which caused Western man to split his nature and designate one part higher, the other lower, has placed beyond our reach the truly religious attitude toward manifestations of sex energy. Our clinically oriented sexologists may indeed succeed in leading contemporary man out of the jungle of old fears to a rational acceptance of sex as a physiological function, but they will not be able to restore to him the ecstatic frenzy of the Dionysian attitude. For the foreseeable future it is safe to predict that the once great Priapus, with his upraised phallus, will remain an obscene rather than a sacred symbol.

**V.
SEX ENERGY
IN THE
FUTURE**

THE LIBERATORS

ANY ATTEMPT to look into the future should be preceded by a glance at the past. As regards the attitude of society toward sex, Rattray Taylor distinguished (*Sex in History*) the matriarchal phase, permissive and indulgent, and the patriarchal phase, stern and filled with prohibitions. We in the West are now passing out of the prohibitive phase and into the permissive phase.

To see this we need look back only one hundred years. Between the 1860's and 1960's what a change! The Victorians were so obsessed with the indecency of anything remotely connected with sex that they even clothed the legs of their pianos. They reasoned that the sight of a "naked leg," albeit that of a piece of furniture, might generate such an excess of lust in the loins of some male visitor that a sexual assault on their innocent daughters would result. Although many moderns still seem to suffer from the delusion that some parts of the body are indecent we can certainly claim to have outgrown the negative sex obsession that resulted in the clothing of piano legs. We can view, on any bathing beach, the entire expanse of the female leg from toes to outlying pubic hairs without any noticeable change in our behavior. The breast is being publicly bared with increasing abandon. Even the upper quadrant of the *gluteus maximus* is allowed to peek coyly over the top of absurdly abbreviated diapers. After being wrapped and bundled until it resembled a bolster the human body has been

204 ← SEX ENERGY IN THE FUTURE

liberated. Along with the restrictive clothing we have shed many fetters of the mind.

It is appropriate at this point to offer praises to those who, at some hazard to themselves, helped to bring about this healthful revolution. Many would place the name of Sigmund Freud at the head of the list of liberators. This probably involves giving to the father of psychoanalysis more credit than he deserves. It would be dishonest, however, to deny that Freud helped to liberate Eros from the slime in which the love god had been covered by the flood tide of the Guilt Cult. Though ill-tempered, narrow-minded and often unscientific, Freud was fearlessly honest about sexual matters at a time when such honesty was not at all acceptable. He saw in sex energy the great fount of creativity, biological and artistic. He saw also the disastrous results of the misapplication of this energy. His great triad, ego, superego and id, provided a key to much that was formerly unintelligible in human behavior. He was instrumental in disposing of the image of the human child as a little sinless angel and proving that sexuality, though not centered in the genitals, is a biological force at work even in the infant.

No doubt Freud overemphasized the role of sex energy in patterning human behavior. He also tended to generalize from inadequate observations. But he opened a window and let a draft of badly needed fresh air into the stuffy spiritual atmosphere that had enveloped Western man as a result of decades of Victorian hypocrisy. He was considerably aided in this endeavor by the labors of Havelock Ellis and Krafft-Ebing who explored the more unusual manifestations of sex energy formerly called perversions, now termed paraphilia.

The liberation of Eros was not solely the work of physicians. The poet William Blake was hurling his denunciations against the black priest of the Guilt Cult as long ago as 1788.

> Children of the future Age
> Reading this indignant page,

Know that in a former time
Love! sweet love, was thought a crime.

Let the Priests of the Raven of dawn no longer, in deadly black, with hoarse note curse the sons of joy. Nor his accepted brethren—whom, tyrant, he calls free—lay the bound or build the roof. Nor pale religious lechery call that virginity that wishes but acts not!
For everything that lives is Holy.

This poetic attack was taken up again more than half a century later by Walt Whitman who, hurling his own brand of defiance at the forces of the Guilt Cult and the sexual hypocrisy of his fellow Americans, sang "the body electric," without omitting the genitals or their products.

From pent-up aching rivers,
From that of myself without which I were nothing,
From what I am determined to make illustrious, even
      if I stand sole among men,
From my own voice resonant, singing the phallus,
Singing the song of procreation.
Singing the need of superb children and therein
            superb grown people,
Singing the muscular urge and the blending,
Singing the bedfellows' song.

The attack on hypocrisy was carried forward by writers as well as poets. Richard Burton, translator of the *Arabian Nights,* founded the Kama Shastra Society of London and Benares in 1882 for the purpose of informing Western man of the sane and honest attitude taken toward sex in the East. The *Kama Sutra,* Vatsyayana's famous manual of sexual love, had been translated by Burton from the Sanskrit in 1876. Now, through the Kama Shastra Society, it was made available to the reading public. It was considered, along with the *Ananga Ranga* and *The Perfumed Garden of the Chiekh Nefzaoui,* one of the most titillating items of Oriental pornography. Actually the *Kama Sutra* is "tender, sage and domestic," to use the words of Burton's most recent biographer.[56] It devotes particular attention to the importance of not frightening the newly wedded bride and recommends that the bridegroom avoid actual sexual union until at least ten days after marriage. "Women have a gentle and timid nature, and they want to be approached with gentleness and consideration. If they are subjected to a brutal assault by a man they hardly know they are apt to conceive a hatred of the sexual act and even sometimes a deep hatred of the entire male sex." This worthy treatise was translated by Burton with a skill and good taste, so much so that, when, in 1962, the book was formally published and made freely available, reviewers, accustomed to far stronger stuff, expressed amazement that it should for so long have been regarded as pornographic.

Indeed the *Kama Sutra* was tepid stuff compared to Burton's next and most famous effort, a translation from the Arabic of the entire *Thousand Nights and a Night* with nothing omitted and a galaxy of footnotes so abundant that they constitute a book within a book. These, along with an essay on the sexual education of women and an 18,000-word account of pederasty in various parts of the world, embodied Burton's vast knowledge of exotic sexual practices and added enormously to the interest of the book.

Oddly enough, although Havelock Ellis's volume on sexual inversion, published in 1898, was prosecuted and the printer heavily fined, Burton's huge work (sixteen volumes), published thirteen years earlier, escaped the censors. Though several editors expressed outrage it was generally praised. Indeed the New York *Tribune* called it "a monument of knowledge and audacity." The success of the book evoked from Burton sarcastic comments on the public taste. He was old and disillusioned. One sees him, in a photograph in Fawn Brodie's book, seated under a tree in a white beaver hat like a sour but unrepentant Dionysus, while his wife stands above him, all bundled in black, waving a forefinger, the very embodiment of Victorian prudery. He gave the poor woman a difficult time but she had her revenge. Scarcely had he breathed his last before she burned all his vast collection of observations on human sexuality, including his new and annotated translation of *The Perfumed Garden.*

Less successful at breaching the prudery barrier but fully as courageous was Frank Harris whose autobiography, *My Life and Loves,* has only recently become available to the general reader. Harris's book is a perfect example of what the Kronhausens, in *Pornography and the Law,* define as erotic realism (as opposed to "hard-core pornography"). It portrays, frankly and simply, the whole life of a man, sexual and otherwise. To the objective reader it is a fascinating picture of England and America at the turn of the century and much of it has nothing to do with sex. But Harris differed from countless other biographers in that he refused to emasculate himself. He loved many women and he described that love, fully, accurately and unashamedly. He did not stop at the kiss and leave the rest to the imagination but detailed the sexual act as it happened, including its less romantic aspects such as the bloodstains on the sheets after he deflowered a virgin.

"I have always fought for the Holy Spirit of Truth and have been, as Heine said he was, a brave soldier in the Liberation War of humanity; now one more fight, the best and the last." It was a fight indeed. Mr. Justice Levy found it necessary to read but a few passages of *My Life and Loves* "to arrive at the inevitable conclusion that it is neither literature nor art." It remained on the black list, available only in Paris, until republished by Grove Press in 1963.

To the names of Burton and Harris must be added those of Henry Miller and D. H. Lawrence, both of them harassed for describing freely the sexual function. Courage also has been shown by Wayland Young who, in his *Eros Denied,*[49] has come to grips with logophobia, the fear of the "dirty word." One of the strangest manifestations of the obscenity delusion is the idea that words in themselves have magical power and that two words, each describing the same thing, may be of quite different orders of "dirtiness." Thus "to fuck" is dirtier than "to copulate," "prick" is dirtier than "penis," "cunt" is dirtier than "vagina," and so on. Even the Kronhausens, whom one would hardly suspect of squeamishness, found it necessary to use circumlocutions like "vernacular for the female sex organ" when quoting excerpts from pornographic books. Yet these very authors point out the absurdity of regarding as obscene an Anglo-Saxon monosyllable while accepting a Latin polysyllable having the same meaning. They quote with approval an editorial from the *Psychiatric Quarterly* in which the subject was dealt with poetically as follows:

Ode to the Four-Letter Word

Oh perish the use of the four-letter words
Whose meanings are never obscure;
The Angles and Saxons, those bawdy old birds,
Were vulgar, obscene and impure.
But cherish the use of the weaseling phrase
That never says quite what you mean.
You had better be known for your hypocrite ways
Than vulgar, impure and obscene.

ANONYMOUS

"All of us know what those words are," adds this editorial. "Most of us learned them as children. All of us have seen them in public or school toilets. Anybody so squeamish as to shudder at them or at the desires or actions toward which they point has no business in psychiatry or psychotherapy."

Prominent among the liberators are those courageous women, Marie Stopes and Margaret Sanger, who struggled for so long against prejudice and the forces of the Guilt Cult to save women from the burden of excessive progeny. Though not directly concerned with Eros they could hardly avoid dealing with the details of sexual intercourse and discussing quite frankly the various factors involved in bringing the sperm into union with the egg. The resistance still exerted against any attempt to regulate conception by the ministers of the Guilt Cult shows the enormous gap that exists between the scientific spirit and the unrealistic dogmas of this dismal religion.

The efforts of all those liberators made it possible for Kinsey and his co-workers to publish that monumental compilation of statistics which reflects the patterns of sexual behavior in America as they were between 1938 and 1952. For this achievement the authors were neither jailed nor reviled. Indeed they were encouraged and the Institute of Sex Research at the University of Indiana continues the sexual research that was started by its founder. Masters and Johnson, in launching their assault on "science's sole timidity," were no doubt encouraged by the reception accorded the Kinsey studies. Though the worshipper of Eros may criticize their efforts as too coldly clinical no advocate of sane sexuality can fail to welcome such studies. Indeed there is no other way to conduct such research, for objective measurements of sexual response must inevitably be concerned with physiological phenomena, the size of the penis, the expansion of the vagina, heart rate, respiration rate, muscular tension, etc. Description of the various raptures that may accompany the act lie in the realm of novelists and poets. Like mystical experiences, which they resemble, the most meaningful sexual experiences defy verbal description.

SEX EDUCATION

Sexual education is the greatest challenge confronting our Western communities. As they gradually emerge from the shadow of the Guilt Cult they seek uncertainly for guideposts through the fog that still remains. Even today, in the United States, in spite of the efforts of the liberators and the obviously urgent need for practical instruction of a youthful population that reaches puberty earlier than ever before, nothing is done to fill this gap. The young are educated in everything except the use of that biological function on which the very existence of the race depends.

This is an age of revolt but today, in the West at least, political revolt is no longer fashionable. No one has much use for the tired clichés of the Marxists. The fervor of the Fascists died with the Führer. The real revolt, which is likely to grow in power as the years go by, is the revolt of the adolescents, of the so-called teen-agers. A muddled and disorganized society, severed from its traditions and lacking an inner aim, has placed the people in this age group in an absurd situation. It treats them neither as children nor as adults. It ignores their biological needs, entangles them in legal jargon which regards as rational such concepts as "statutory rape" and "undermining the morals of a minor." It sets up artificial age limits and ignores the biological difference between the sexual need of the male and that of the female. Furthermore it immerses the members of this age group in the old morass of hypocrisy and fraud, centering around a phony concept of "youthful innocence" already thoroughly debunked by Freud and Company, not to mention Kinsey *et al.*

We should emphasize here that the flood of sentimental hogwash, centering around the concept of "protecting childish innocence," did not inundate the spirit of Western man until quite recently. Medieval society, Phillipe Aries informs us in *Centuries of Childhood*,[57] made no attempt to shield its children from witnessing that event which later writers have called the "primal scene." Adults had sexual relations before the children and watched with indulgent amusement when the little ones attempted to follow their elders' example. Wrote Aries: "The idea did not yet exist that reference to sexual matters could soil childish innocence; nobody thought that this innocence really existed. It was not until the eighteenth or nineteenth century that the wall developed between child and adult and the unhappy youngster was torn out of his home to be uniformed, underfed and flogged by pretentious pedagogues in gaunt establishments such as those described by Dickens with all the attributes of prisons but which masqueraded under the name of boarding schools."

Today a sophisticated skeptical generation, raised in the shadow of the H-bomb and confronted daily with the spectacle of the idiocy of its elders, is likely to revolt with vigor against the inadequacies of its sexual education. Weary of restrictions imposed by a muddled morality in the name of a god who is generally conceded to be dead, they will demand with increasing insistence their biological rights. "For how much longer are we expected to struggle with our urgent sexual desires as if they were some sort of disease? Why must we channel our vigorous erotic impulses into fantasies? Why must we grope and guess instead of learning the arts of sexual love from those qualified to teach just as one learns any other art?" These are questions they are bound to ask with increasing frequency. They will expect an answer and it had better be a valid one.

What is a valid answer? It is not for a biologist to cope with matters of morality. Certainty regarding right and wrong is granted only to Papists and Maoists. The biologist can only offer alternatives. Leaving the moral pronouncements to priests and commissars he views the problem as a whole, in the light of material provided by other societies, both human and sub-human. It is helpful first to take a look at the sex lives of apes and monkeys. Though these "lower forms" cannot claim to be "conquerors of space" or "masters of the atom," in many respects they manage their affairs far better than does man.

So what do the monkeys teach regarding sexuality? One thing above all, as the studies of Dr. H. F. Harlow have shown. Sexual behavior in the primates (apes and monkeys) is something they learn by imitation of their elders. The sexual urge is instinctive (unlearned) but the channeling of that urge into appropriate patterns of behavior depends on education. Dr. Harlow's monkeys which had been raised in isolation were totally lacking in sexual know-how. The males tried to mount the females head first or approached them from the side. Some of the monkeys raised in solitude showed no interest in sexual intercourse at all. As Dr. Harlow put it, they had done everything possible to create a disease-free colony of monkeys by raising the animals in isolation only to find that they had produced not a breeding colony but a brooding colony. These observations apply specifically to the male. The female primate seems equipped by nature to fulfill her sexual role without education.

The evidence indicates that young apes and monkeys learn the art of sexual intercourse from their elders. The adults copulate, the little ones imitate. There is, among these so-called lower animals, no talk of "lewd and lascivious conduct" or of "undermining the morals of a minor." Sex education among monkeys is accepted as a part of the general preparation for living, which includes learning where to find food and how to avoid foes. Only man, an insanely muddled monster seemingly headed for self-annihilation, has managed to become so entangled in his own taboos that he regards practical sex education of the young as immoral.

Beach and Ford also observe that among subhuman primates it is the male who is most dependent on sexual learning. Of the human they write: ". . . if they are ever to derive maximal satisfaction from sexual relations, individuals who are reared under conditions that prevent or seriously reduce experimentation and practice during childhood and adolescence will be forced to go through the essential learning process after adulthood has been attained.

"This type of adjustment may be exceedingly difficult for young adults of either sex, particularly if they belong to a society that inculcates manifold sexual inhibitions in the developing individual. The man or woman who learned during childhood and adolescence that it was 'wrong' to examine or stimulate his or her own genitals, that it was even 'worse' to have any contact with those of another person, and, particularly, that attempts at heterosexual relations were immoral, is expected to reverse completely at least some of these attitudes on the wedding night or shortly thereafter. This expectation is difficult to fulfill. If the initial lessons have been well learned, the unlearning is bound to take a long time and may never be completed." [17]

PERMISSIVE PATTERN

The above reproach cannot be applied to all human societies. In their survey (*Patterns of Sexual Behavior*),[17] Beach and Ford list thirty-two human societies which take "a completely tolerant and permissive attitude toward sex expression in childhood." Among the Chewa of Africa, these authors inform us, it is believed that unless children exercise themselves sexually early in life they will never beget offspring. Little huts are built some distance from the village and in these the boys and girls play at being husband and wife with the knowledge and complete approval of their parents. The trial matings extend into adolescence with periodic changes of partners until finally marriage occurs. Similarly, among the Ila-speaking peoples of Africa, childhood is regarded as a time of preparation for mature sexual functions. Each girl is given a house to which she takes the boy of her choice. There they play as man and wife. "It is reported that there are no virgins among these people after the age of ten."

The Ifugao of the Philippines permit each boy to sleep with a girl every night. "The only check on promiscuity is that imposed by the girls themselves. Usually a girl is unwilling to form too prolonged an attachment to one boy until she is ready to be married. Boys are urged by their fathers to begin sexual activities early, and a man may shame his son if the latter is backward in this respect.

"The Lepcha of India believe that girls will not mature without benefit of sexual intercourse. Early sex play among boys and girls characteristically involves many forms of mutual masturbation and usually ends in attempted copulation. By the time they are eleven or twelve years old, most girls regularly engage in full intercourse. Older men occasionally copu-

late with girls as young as eight years of age. Instead of being
regarded as a criminal offense, such behavior is considered
amusing by the Lepcha. Sexual life begins in earnest among
the Trobrianders at six or eight years for girls, ten to twelve
for boys. Both sexes receive explicit instruction from older
companions whom they imitate in sex activities. Sex play
includes masturbation, oral stimulation of the genitals of the
same and opposite sex, and heterosexual copulation. At any
time a couple may retire to the bush, the bachelor's hut, an
isolated yam house, or any other convenient place and there
engage in prolonged sexual play with the full approval of their
parents. No marriage is consummated in Trobriand society
without a protracted preliminary period of sexual intimacy
during which both sincerity of affection and sexual compati-
bility are tested. Premarital pregnancy is said to be rare in this
society, despite postpuberal sexual intercourse over a period
of three years or more before marriage. This experience has led
the Trobrianders to doubt a causal relationship between coitus
and conception. Instead they consider supernatural influences
to be far more significant in causing a child to be conceived.

"In this instance, as in other cases of frequent but infertile
coitus among postpubescent males and females, the phenomenon of adolescent sterility would appear to be particularly
pertinent. It may well be that although they have passed the
menarche, the girls involved in this activity are not yet ovu-
lating, or at least are incapable of carrying a fetus to term.
Any such interpretation must remain speculative, however,
until there is more satisfactory proof for the absence of any
form of contraception." [17]

For Western man the permissive pattern of sexual behavior
is generally associated with Polynesia. Ever since Captain
Cook published his first accounts of beauties with brown
bodies and flashing teeth who swam out to the ships of the
white men and embraced the sailors, the South Sea Island
societies have been regarded as the embodiment of sexual
permissiveness. This was the first glimpse Western man had

had of pure sexuality uncontaminated by guilt since the cult of Dionysus was replaced by that of the Cross. Things have certainly changed since the days of Captain Cook. The flashing teeth have fallen victims to the spirochete of syphilis. The Dionysian sexuality has lost much of its vigor, restrained by tight-trousered ministers of the Guilt Cult. The blight of the white man has spread across the Pacific.

Even so the pattern has not disappeared. Writing of contemporary Polynesia, James Michener (*Return to Paradise*) describes Bora Bora as "an island where girls loved to have babies which they could give to older couples who had no children, where fathers built their daughters separate cabins so they could be alone for their courting." The adolescent, male or female, was free to indulge in unrestricted sexual intercourse, provided he or she avoided relatives. The fruits of the intercourse were adopted gladly. After a girl had borne one or two children on this basis she was ready for marriage, having proved to the satisfaction of her spouse that she was not sterile. The ridiculous concept of the illegitimate child did not even exist.

HETAERA PATTERN

The hetaera pattern of sexual education is extremely old and was considered perfectly normal and respectable in such cultures as that of ancient Greece. This resulted from a completely different attitude to what we nowadays call prostitution. To the Greeks of the age of Pericles a woman could either be a wife and a mother or a courtesan. And the courtesan, like the geisha of Japan, was expected to be a mistress not only of the fine art of love but also of many other arts that gladden the hearts of men and take their minds off their worries.

"Many of them are distinguished by refined education and a quick wit at repartee," wrote Helbig of the hetaerae of ancient Greece. "They know how to fascinate the most distinguished personalities of their time—generals, statesmen, men of letters and artists, and how to keep their affection; they illustrate in the manner indicated a mixed existence of fine intellectual and sensual pleasures, to which the majority of Greeks at that time paid homage. In the life of almost every important person-ality, prominent in the history of Hellenism, the influence of well-known hetaerae can be proved. Most of their contempo-raries found nothing offensive in it. In the time of Polybius the most beautiful houses in Alexandria were named after famous flute-players and hetaerae. Portrait statues of such women were set up on the temples and other public buildings by the side of those of meritorious generals and statesmen." [58]

If such distinguished ladies were beyond the limited means of the adolescents of antiquity there were always the cheaper grades of female flesh who sat at the doors of what the Romans called *lupanaria* and who would sell their services for as little as an obol. Why should hot youths commit adultery, asks Athenaeus, with all the risks that such behavior involves? Are there not enough comely girls in the brothels? "One can look at them and see how, with bared breasts and in thin dresses of gauze, they exhibit themselves in the sun. Any youth can pick out the one that pleases him—thin, fat, roundish, lanky, crooked, young, old, medium, mature. No need to set up a ladder and enter secretly. No need to creep in through the dormer window, or cleverly smuggle yourself in in a heap of straw. They themselves drag you almost with violence into the house, calling you, if you are already an old man, 'daddy,' otherwise 'little brother' or 'little youngster.' You can have any one of them for a small sum without risk by day or toward evening."

In ancient Rome it was so completely taken for granted that the young man would direct his lust into this pattern of sexual behavior that even the stern Cato did not object to it. Says Horace, in the satire in which he speaks of sexual life: "When a very famous man had visited a brothel, he said: Praised to eternity be the sensible opinion of old Cato. As soon as desire brings the blood in the veins of young men to boiling heat, it is right and just that they should go this way and not seduce respectable married women."

Times have changed since the days of Horace. The American Catos, with their Puritan backgrounds and high index of hypocrisy, have ruled out anything like the honest sexual fellowship provided by hetaerae or geishas at social get-togethers in ancient Greece or contemporary Japan. Even the simple satisfaction of animal needs which the youth of Rome obtained in the *lupanaria* is nowadays so befogged with guilt and fear that this form of indulgence may have lasting harmful effects. Several instances are reported by the Kronhausens (*Sex Histories of American College Men*).[59] For the adolescent, they state, an attempt to obtain satisfaction from a prostitute may prove a devastating experience. One thinks of Holden Caulfield's misery on being confronted in a cheap hotel with the squalid realities of commercialized sex (*The Catcher in the Rye*). The situation described by Salinger occurs all too frequently in real life. "An unfortunate first experience of this kind can, of course, have long-lasting effects, and may even result in potency difficulties." [59]

In countries less given to sexual hypocrisy than the United States the hetaera relationship can still prove satisfactory. "In Japan," states another of the Kronhausens' subjects, "I found the girls tender and considerate, as well as clean, and I honestly enjoyed myself in their company. . . . As far as the prostitutes in the U.S. are concerned, I consider them among the lowest creatures and could not ever have anything to do with them."

TEA AND SYMPATHY PATTERN

This is a pattern of sexual behavior which already exists in our society and may become more prevalent. The Kronhausens, in their study already quoted, have devoted a whole chapter to its description. The title applied to this pattern of sex education is taken from the play of this name by R. W. Anderson. The dramatic action centers around the predicament of young Tom Lee. Accused of homosexuality the lad tries to clear himself of suspicion and prove himself sexually adequate by attempting intercourse with a tough young whore, an attempt which proves a shattering fiasco. He is finally rescued from his disastrous emotional turmoil by the wife of his headmaster who supplies him not only with tea but also with a gentle initiation into those sexual mysteries which, up to that point, have held for him so much terror.

The Kronhausens indicate that this form of sex education is already quite prevalent on college campuses and is likely to become more so. It offers many of the advantages of the hetaera or geisha relationship without its drawbacks. To the romantically minded American who exaggerates some aspects of sexual relations while he hides from others, "young love" has long been a symbol of something glorious and golden, an idyllic state of affairs the delights of which, in a highly bowdlerized form, are described in innumerable articles in the women's magazines. But many of the college men interviewed by the Kronhausens described their experiences with young love as anything but idyllic. To the girl's almost inevitable sense of guilt and fear of pregnancy was added an awkwardness resulting from complete ignorance of the practice of sex relations. Several of these youths, who had found prostitutes revolting and young girls too difficult, were rescued from their dilemma by older women, sometimes married, sometimes not, who knew what they were doing, could be trusted to take care of themselves and brought to the sexual act a certain lightness very different from the overheated emotionalism, compounded of lust and fear, with which the act becomes imbued when two virginities meet. Said one of the Kronhausens' subjects: "There was joking involved, a congeniality and willingness which seemed wonderful to me—so much more satisfying and natural than the great show of emotion that went into necking and petting with the college kids with the gasps and sighs . . . so phony and false." [59]

In this willingness of older or at any rate sexually mature women to undertake the initiation of youths into the mystery of sex the Kronhausens see evidence of the great sexual revolution which "is perhaps progressing at a much faster rate on the college campus than on Main Street." The American female has thrown off her passivity and is showing an aggressiveness in matters sexual that startles Mother and horrifies Granny. The male, it appears, has not had quite enough time to adjust himself to this state of affairs and tends to shrink from the overwhelming female, like those pathetic figures with toothbrush moustaches which the late James Thurber so loved to depict. To the nervous and fumbling youth, however, this willingness on the part of the female to take the initiative may prove a blessing.

The female of the species, besides being, as Kipling assures us, more deadly than the male, may also be less of a hypocrite. The sexual emancipation which has progressed so far in the Scandinavian countries appears to have been largely the work of women. So the mature and emancipated college female, married or single, may lead the way to a realization that there is much of both art and science in the practice of sexual love; that, as so much of human happiness depends on harmonious and full sex relationships, practical instruction in this aspect of behavior should be part of the education of every youth and maiden. We may yet see, as the clouds of the Guilt Cult slowly thin to admit a little sunlight, the establishment of Professorships of Applied Sexuality occupied by professors, both male and female, chosen for their understanding of the erotic arts.

BRAVE NEW WORLD PATTERN

The pattern of sex education described by Aldous Huxley in *Brave New World* [60] represents present-day tendencies taken to their logical conclusions. Stable pair groups are out. Monogamy is a thing of the past. The husband-wife pair, fettered to each other like convicts in a chain gang, are no longer in evidence. No longer are parents entrusted with the raising of the young, a task for which, in many cases, they are hopelessly ill-equipped. There are no parents anyway, and the words father and mother have become obscene. Sexual intercourse is no longer associated with reproduction, the latter process being carried out scientifically on warmed microscope slides whereon the genetically selected sperm meets the no less genetically selected egg to produce a human being whose level of intelligence is more or less predictable.

Even the scientifically oriented modern might feel that planning in *Brave New World* has been taken a little too far and that too many things of value have been sacrificed in the interest of stability. But the objective observer can hardly fail to admit that sex education in that hypothetical society makes more sense than the hopelessly haphazard approach that prevails at the moment in Western societies which consider themselves progressive. Erotic play among the very young is accepted and encouraged as a natural healthy manifestation. (Poor little kids! exclaim the students when informed by their teacher of the amazing fact that an earlier culture branded these activities as immoral.) Such play, however, is only a beginning. As puberty approaches more and more time is devoted to education in the art and science of applied sexuality. This training includes, for the girls, Malthusian Drill; instruction in the application of contraceptive methods. A belt containing the regulation supply of contraceptives is an integral part of the equipment of every fertile female. If contraception fails there are always the Abortion Centers which, far from being gloomy places full of shadows of guilt and sin, are recognized adjuncts to civilized life and floodlighted on Tuesdays and Fridays.

As a result of these arrangements, the adolescents of *Brave New World* have no sexual problems. Passing without any frustrating delays from juvenile sex play to the pleasures of complete coition they scamper from partner to partner with fewer taboos to bother about than even the brown adolescents of Bora Bora.

No wonder the teen-agers brought up under these circumstances could hardly believe their ears when told of the sexual continence forcibly imposed on their unhappy predecessors.

> "Even adolescents," the D. H. C. was saying, "even adolescents like yourselves . . ."
>
> "Not possible!"
>
> "Barring a little surreptitious autoerotism and homosexuality—absolutely nothing."
>
> "Nothing?"
>
> "In most cases, till they were over twenty years old."
>
> "Twenty years old?" echoed the students in a chorus of loud disbelief.
>
> "Twenty," the Director repeated. "I told you that you'd find it incredible." [60]

THE SANE SEX SOCIETY

Changes become possible only when those involved demand a change, demand it vigorously, clamorously and obstreperously. Yesterday the proletariat were the injured ones, today the teen-agers. Preached at, deplored, dragooned, deprived, the males herded into camps to be butchered in senseless wars before they have even the right to vote, the females encouraged to play the role of women without being permitted to function sexually, it is hardly surprising that this segment of the population seethes with resentment, acts defiantly, takes drugs, runs away from home, wears beards, long hair and generally plays the rebel.

". . . our society does not like them," writes Wayland Young of the teen-agers. "It keeps a nice little cautery stuck into their vitals. They must not fuck, which is as much as to say that they must not be what they are. We feed them well with one hand and make them healthy; with the other we block them off from the waist down. We show them movies in which people kiss, and never move their pelvises. We make great proclamations about the deep and satisfying fidelities which some of us are lucky enough to wake up one day when we are about forty and find are what we turn out to have, but to young people it only means: 'Don't.' We tell the boy: 'Respect your girl.' She weeps. We tell the girl: 'Your boy will respect you if you say no.' He turns away sneering. Hope wilts, and love is stillborn." [49]

If we simply urge continence before marriage without informing our teen-agers of the real situation, we infringe their human freedom, and trick them.

"At present our society does, broadly speaking, trick teen-agers in this way. If they fuck casually in doorways and in cars it is because we take good care they shall have nowhere else. If they go to twenty-dollar abortionists it is because we keep contraceptives from them, especially from the girls. If in their general attitude they seem set against society it is because society is so set against them. We work off our guilts on them, just as we do on the prostitute. The prostitute exists for sex, and carries on her back a good part of our conviction that sex is a bad thing. Young people, whether they are married or not, are more sexually active than the middle-aged and carry the rest.

"There are great, creaking anachronisms at large in our sexual morality today, injunctions and prohibitions which once had meaning and function, but are now left without, high and dry, and generate resentment and depression; these are the dead shreds of Manichaeism and libertinism which I called the Cheshire scowl and the Cheshire leer. The former is the stronger. They generate resentment and depression by themselves, since the religious struggles which created them and gave them meaning are now over. But more than that there have been changes in the structure of society in this century, and in industrial technology, which make these anachronisms doubly hurtful; not only have they no meaning any longer, they are bedeviling a kind of people who did not formerly exist at all."

No matter what pattern of sex education is finally accepted by modern human societies it will have to take into account the population explosion. The obvious fact that the earth's surface can support only a limited number of human beings makes regulation of population density essential. The methods that can be used are three in number, infanticide, abortion and contraception. In a sentimentalized society that insists on raising every child that is born including imbeciles, idiots, morons and monsters, infanticide is not very likely to prove acceptable. Abortion, though accepted in such countries as Japan, is still frowned upon in many so-called enlightened countries whose members, though they do not hesitate to plan the murder of millions, make a great deal of fuss over the termination of the life of a four-inch fetus.

There remains contraception. This procedure, though defined as sinful by certain ecclesiastics who dwell in a world that is far removed from the real one, is the most acceptable method of population control. A combination of Polynesian permissiveness with reliable contraceptive methods seems the procedure most likely to become adopted in the future. If parents still insist on pretending that their teen-aged children are sexually unawakened and therefore should not be given contraceptive devices, an increasingly rebellious generation of adolescents will simply take matters into its own hands and seek information (and protection) elsewhere.

Grandiose talk of the Great Society sounds increasingly hollow to those who have newly reached puberty, in whose bodies the sexual ferment works most powerfully but whose normal outlets are blocked by the collective Cheshire scowl of the adult world, incarnated in flat-footed police officers, male and female, empowered to drag young lovers into court on the charge of corrupting one another's morals. This state of affairs can be changed only if adult members of society, remembering the storms and stress of their own sexually frustrated adolescence, are willing to exert some pressure on those who fashion the laws.

The Sane Sex Society was founded by those who believe that practical education in sexual activity is necessary for members of both sexes if they are later to fulfill their roles as mates and parents. The guilt-filled, anxiety-ridden gropings of two adolescents neither of whom knows what he or she is doing must be replaced by a calm, affectionate initiation, in the course of which the young learn the arts of sexual love without fear and without guilt. So warped, however, are the attitudes of this society that he who suggests that older women initiate boys and older men teach girls is at once accused of the grossest immorality, though this pattern of sexual behavior is obviously less fraught with perils than letting the young find things out for themselves by trial and error (error which may have a disastrous effect on their future lives).

The Sane Sex Society proclaims as a self-evident truth that the teen-ager is as much entitled to normal gratification of his sexual impulses as is the so-called adult, that there is no biological justification for legislation that penalizes sexual intercourse because one or both partners happen to be under the age of eighteen. Such legislation falls in the category of cruel and unusual punishments and, for this reason, should be ruled unconstitutional.

This legislation arises out of the proposition that the teen-ager should be protected from lecherous adults eager to take advantage of the youngster's innocence. But it is precisely this innocence (by which is meant ignorance) that most endangers the teen-ager. There is no evidence to show that young girls who have been taught by older men, or boys who have been initiated by older women, suffered harmful consequences as a result, provided the relationship was affectionate and not too possessive. Humbert Humbert's disastrous effect on Lolita and her no less disastrous effect on H. H. was not due to the

discrepancy in their ages but to the frantic almost insane pos-
sessiveness of the older man whose intelligence should have
told him that he could never "possess" his nymphet, that his
role was only that of a teacher of the art of love, and that her
permanent mate, if she wanted one, would have to be someone
of her own age group.

Real sexual education will not become possible until the
"armor" (to use Wilhelm Reich's term) [61] which artificially
blocks the flow of biological forces in the body is shed by those
who make the laws that are intended to govern our sexual
behavior. We no longer, as did our Victorian forebears, stran-
gle and stifle our bodies with corsets and crinolines. We have
learned to expose our bodies to the sun and air almost as freely
as did the Spartans of old. We have proved less proficient in
freeing ourselves of mental corsets. It is still difficult for contemporary man, who lives largely in his head, to accept freely
the messages that arrive from his pelvic regions. He is blocked
off from these impulses by old fears and superstitions. Though
he has usually outgrown his ancestor's belief in demonic powers he still refuses to accept sex energy as a life-giving force
which must be allowed to flow freely and vitalize the entire
body. He wants to hide it in a box, block it off, fetter it with
legal restrictions. He is afraid of it.

He cannot keep this fear to himself but proceeds to teach
it to his children, thus ensuring that they too will be armored
and biologically maimed. The natural impulse of the child to
explore its own body is inhibited almost before the child is out
of diapers. The whole pelvic region is placed "off limits" perhaps before the child is six years old. Sensations associated
with sex and defecation alike become surrounded with an aura
of the forbidden. They are "dirty." They are also unmention-
able. One may not talk about them and one should not think
about them. Thus the block is formed and, once formed, is
hard to remove. Full sexual response becomes impossible as
long as the block remains.

It is this block that stands in the way of any real progress toward sexual education. Practical sex education means sex experience. It does not mean discreet little talks about birds and bees, or even about penises and vaginas. Man's intellectual brain, a presumptuous mechanism forever trying to perform functions for which it was never intended, can never come to a proper understanding of the uses of sex energy. To be properly used, this force must be allowed to flow freely, to take over the body and express itself in its own way. Sex energy expresses itself through the whole of the organism. The healing, revitalizing effect of the sexual orgasm cannot be exerted if the energy is blocked off at any level of the body. Wilhelm Reich is surely correct in asserting that as long as such blockage exists real psychological health is unattainable.[61]

In a society the population of which consists largely of blocked individuals, true sex education for the young will always be opposed. Those who have spent their whole lives in bondage come to fear freedom. They love their chains and try to hand on those chains to their descendants. Progress might be hastened if those who have managed to liberate themselves would work together, form a Sane Sex Society dedicated to removing the obstacles now standing in the way of practical sex education for the young. Members of such a society would draw attention to the biological needs of those to whom the law insists on referring as minors. They would point out that there is no mysterious borderline separating adults from adolescents, that the sexual needs of the latter are as urgent as those of the former, that an adult who initiates an adolescent into the art of sexual love is not, if she does it wisely, contributing to the delinquency of a minor. Rather, she is contributing a badly needed element in that person's education.

The powerful forces of the Guilt Cult still rampant in our culture make it certain that the future history of the Sane Sex Society will be colorful. Passions of quite extraordinary virulence are aroused as soon as anyone dares suggest that knowledge is better than a phony innocence and that satisfying patterns of sexual behavior can and should be taught as part of the general education of every teen-ager. It remains to be seen whether the members of our culture can ever really free themselves from the residue of centuries of sexual guilt. The process of emergence from this swamp is bound to be an uphill struggle. Many setbacks are to be expected before this society, so confident of its superiority, emerges from the gloomy jungles of the past and gives to sex energy its rightful place as the greatest of vivifying and uplifting forces.

References

1. Shettles, L. B., *Ovum Humanum* (New York: Hafner, 1961).
2. Fabre, J. H. C., *The Life and Love of the Insect* (London: A. C. Black, 1918).
3. Maeterlinck, M., *The Life of the Bee* (New York: Dodd, Mead and Co., 1936).
4. Marais, E., *The Soul of the White Ant* (London: Methuen and Co., 1937).
5. Escherich, K., *Die Termiten oder weissen Ameisen* (Leipzig: W. Klinkhardt, 1909).
6. Maeterlinck, M., *The Life of the Ant* (New York: The John Day Co., 1930).
7. Wendt, H., *The Sex Life of the Animals* (New York: Simon and Schuster, 1965).
8. Lorenz, K., *King Solomon's Ring: New Light on Animal Ways* (New York: T. Y. Crowell Co., 1952).
9. Beebe, W., *High Jungle* (New York: Duell, Sloan and Pearce, 1949).
10. Ardrey, R., *The Territorial Imperative* (New York: Atheneum, 1966).
11. Schein, M. W., and E. B. Hale, "Stimuli Eliciting Sexual Behavior," in *Sex and Behavior*, Frank A. Beach, editor (New York: John Wiley and Sons, 1965).
12. Rothschild, M., "Fleas," *Scientific American*, December, 1965, p. 44.
13. Michelmore, S., *Sexual Reproduction* (New York: The Natural History Press, 1964).
14. Wilson, E. O., "Pheromones," *Scientific American*, May, 1963, p. 100.
15. Bolsche, W., *Love Life in Nature: The Story of the Evolution of Love* (London: J. Cape, 1931).

16. Hediger, H., "Environmental Factors Influencing the Reproduction of Zoo Animals," in *Sex and Behavior, op. cit.*
17. Beach, F. A., and Ford, C. S., *Patterns of Sexual Behavior* (New York: Harper Bros., 1951).
18. Masters, W. H., and V. E. Johnson, *Human Sexual Response* (Boston: Little, Brown and Co., 1966).
19. Fisher, A. E., "Chemical Stimulation of the Brain," *Scientific American*, June, 1964, p. 60.
20. Klüver, H., and P. C. Bucy, "Preliminary Analysis of the Functions of the Temporal Lobes in Monkeys," *Archives of Neurology and Psychiatry* 42:979–1000.
21. Schriener, L., and A. Kling, "Behavioral Changes Following Rhinencephalic Injury in Cats," *Journal of Neurophysiology* 16:643–659.
22. Harris, F., *My Life and Loves* (New York: Grove Press, 1963).
23. Masters, W. H., and W. M. Allen, "Investigation of Sexual Rejuvenation of Elderly Women," in *Tenth Conference on Problems of Aging* (Josiah Macy Jr. Foundation, 1948).
24. De Kruif, P. H., *Male Hormone* (New York: Harcourt, Brace, 1945).
25. Durrell, L., *Justine* (New York: Dutton and Co., 1957).
26. Davenport, W., "Sexual Patterns and their Regulation in a Society of the Southwest Pacific," in *Sex and Behavior, op. cit.*
27. Hamilton, G. V., "A Study in Sexual Tendencies in Monkeys and Baboons," *Journal of Animal Behavior* 4:295–318, 1914.
28. Taylor, G. R., *Sex in History* (New York: Vanguard Press, 1954).
29. Knight, R. P., "A Discourse on the Worship of Priapus," in *Sexual Symbolism* (New York: Julian Press, 1957).
30. Kiefer, O., *Sexual Life in Ancient Rome* (London: Routledge and Kegan Paul, 1932).
31. Wright, T., "The Worship of the Generative Powers," in *Sexual Symbolism, op. cit.*
32. Petronius, *Satyricon*, W. Arrowsmith, translator (Ann Arbor: University of Michigan Press, 1959).
33. Seltman, C., *Women in Antiquity* (New York: St. Martin's Press, 1955).
34. Goldberg, B. Z., *The Sacred Fire* (New York: Horace Liveright, 1930).
35. Partridge, B., *A History of Orgies* (New York: Bonanza Books, 1960).

36. Renault, M., *The King Must Die* (New York: Pantheon Books, 1958).

37. *Hatha Yoga Pradipika,* quoted in Bernard, T., *Hatha Yoga* (London: Rider and Co., 1950).

38. *Gheranda Samhita,* quoted in *Hatha Yoga, op. cit.*

39. *Siva Samhita,* quoted in *Hatha Yoga, op. cit.*

40. Eliade, M., *Yoga: Immortality and Freedom* (New York: Pantheon Books, 1958).

41. Huxley, A., *Island* (New York: Harper Bros., 1962).

42. David-Neel, A., *Initiations and Initiates in Tibet* (New York: University Books, 1959).

43. Thomas, P., *Kama Kalpa* (Bombay: Taraporevala Sons, 1960).

44. Apuleius, *The Golden Ass,* Robert Graves, translator (New York: The Pocket Library, 1954).

45. Josephus, F., *The Wars of the Jews* (London: Nelson and Sons, 1883).

46. Masters, R. E. L., *Eros and Evil* (New York: Julian Press, 1962).

47. Huxley, A., *The Devils of Loudon* (New York: Harper Bros., 1952).

48. Bloch, I., *Sexual Life in England* (London: Aldor, 1938).

49. Young, W., *Eros Denied* (New York: Grove Press, 1964).

50. Vatsyayana, *Kama Sutra* (London, Benares: Cosmopoli Kama Shastra Society, 1961).

51. Terrot, P., *Traffic in Innocents* (New York: Dutton and Co., 1960).

52. De Beauvoir, S., "Must we burn Sade?" in *Marquis de Sade* (New York: Grove Press, 1953).

53. Johnson, P. H., *On Iniquity* (New York: Scribners, 1967).

54. Kronhausen, E. and P., *Pornography and the Law* (New York: Ballantine Books, 1959).

55. Maraini, F., *Secret Tibet* (New York: Viking Press, 1952).

56. Brodie, F., *The Devil Drives* (New York: Norton and Co., 1967).

57. Aries, P., *Centuries of Childhood* (New York: Knopf, 1962).

58. Quoted in Licht, H., *Sexual Life in Ancient Greece* (London: Routledge and Kegan Paul, 1932).

59. Kronhausen, E. and P., *Sex Histories of American College Men* (New York: Ballantine Books, 1960).

60. Huxley, A., *Brave New World* (New York: Harper Bros., 1932).

61. Reich, W., *The Function of the Orgasm* (New York: Noonday Press, 1962).

Index

duckbilled platypus, 82
ducks, 69ff.
Durrell, Lawrence, 108, 198

Earth Mother, 131
earth worm, 51
echidna, 82
education, sexual, 209
energy, sex, 33
Eros, 16
Eros and Thanatos, 159
erotic play, 220
estradiol, 103
estrogens, 98, 106

Fabre, Jean Henri, 40ff.
fascinum, 120
Feast of Venus, 185
female sex organ, worship of, 130ff.
fern, 36
flagellation, 180ff.
flea, 74
follicle, 27
Freud, Sigmund, 204
frog, 62ff.

gametes, 15
genetic code, 9
gerenuk, 84
Ginzberg, Ralph, 190
Guilt Cult, 163ff.
    modern, 193ff.
gypsy moth, 78

Harris, Frank, 111f., 207
Hatha Yoga, 144
hell, 177
herbivores, 84

hermaphrodite, 51
hetaera, 215
hormone replacement, 105
hormones, sex, 98ff.
Huxley, Aldous, 219ff.

imprinting, 68
incubi and succubi, 177
insect pollination, 33, 37
insects, 77
Ishtar, 131

jackdaw, 66ff.
jelly fish, 33
Johnson, V. E., 89, 93ff., 107, 196

Kama Sutra, 205
Kali, Cult of, 140
kaula rite, 152
Kinsey, A. C., 93, 196
Kundalini, 144

Lanuvium, phallic procession in, 117
Lawrence, D. H., 207
leech, 37ff.
liberators, 204
life, code of, 6
lizard, 80
logophobia, 207f.
Lorenz, Konrad, 60, 68
lupanaria, 216

macrogamete, 15
macro-sex, 4
maithuna, 89
Malleus Maleficarum, 178
mantis, 42

termite, 48ff.
testosterone, 100, 106
tumescence. *See* orgasm, male;
  orgasm, female
turkey, 69
turtle, 82

uterus, 91ff.

vagina, 91ff.
vajroli, 148

virus, 11ff.

Wendt, Herbert, 53
Whitman, Walt, 205
woman, worship of, 131

yoni, 131ff.
Yoni Mudra, 145

zygospore, 13
zygote, 29